EATING IN
The Official Single Man's Cookbook

RICH LIPPMAN &
JOSÉ MALDONADO

ILLUSTRATED BY
JOE AZAR

YOUR COPY IS
PRE·STAINED
& READY FOR ACTION

Inspected by
Bachelor No. 3

ACKNOWLEDGEMENTS

The authors would like to thank these people for their help, advice and support:

Bill Cates, who turned CorkScrew into a reality; Debra Wolf, who thoughtfully edited out our (most blatant) sexist remarks; Dennis Goris of Bremmer & Goris, who designed EATING IN; Pamela Brown and Barbara Manning, for all their encouragement and patience; plus. . . Randy Anderson, Bruce Brooks, Ron Pottle, Marian Platt, Robin Soslow, David Page, Andrea Mann, Winafred Brantl, Betsy Franklin, Bill Driscoll, Debbie Olan, Bob Spar, Debra Curry, John Gelzer, Neil & Susan, Jim Harmon, Larry Miller, Julia Newhouse, Ed Bongiovani; our parents Ro & Shel, Ida & Guillermo, Joe Cates, Paulette Azar; and all the countless women who endured our cooking—your antidote is in the mail.

Test Kitchens

The authors made every effort to ensure the accuracy of recipes in this book. Please contact these test chefs if your meal turns out weird:

Guy Wilcomb, René Moreno, Mike Mazzone, Michael Groce, Mike Bodary and Will Maldonado.
Brian "Beezer" Lewis, Chief Chef; Robert Luskin & Mike Bitel, Wine Consultants.

Dedicated to the memories of Ben Gold and Tomas Maldonado.

CORKSCREW PRESS

P.O. Box 2691, Silver Spring, MD 20902-0115

Text Copyright ©1988 by Richard A. Lippman and José M. Maldonado
Illustrations Copyright ©1988 by Joseph Azar

ISBN 0-944042-00-7
Library of Congress Number: 88-070598

10 9 8 7 6 5 4
Printed in the U.S.A.

TO SINGLE MEN
who survive daily on Doritos, Ding Dongs and Domino's

AND TO SINGLE WOMEN
who've always been stuck with the cooking and cleaning

THIS IS YOUR LUCKY DAY. . .

EATING IN is cooking up a lot of hot romances:

"THE BEST DINNER DATE I ever had!"

—H.H., engineer

"I COOKED MY FIRST REAL DINNER for one of the women in my office. Now they all *want to come over. Help!"*

—A.L., financial planner

"I PREPARED YOUR 'STEAK (HER NAME HERE)' for a gorgeous woman named Suzanne. When she tasted my 'Steak Suzanne,' she said I could cook for her anytime. And I do!"

—B.D., freelance artist

"I SAVED $10 ON THE WINE and $15 on the food effectively reducing the cost of dating 50% and increasing the quality 100%!"

—D.B., C.P.A.

"I BURNED THE MEAL and smoked out the apartment and she was still thrilled because I tried."

—B.F., landscape architect

"MY GIRLFRIEND WAS SO SURPRISED I had actually cleaned up my apartment, she even lost her fear of using my bathroom.'"

—W.M., letter carrier

EATING IN is picking up a lot of rave reviews:

"EATING IN IS A FUNNY, SEXY and completely well-researched guide for the guy who previously used his kitchen as a place to work on his car."
—Baltimore Sun

"NOT ONLY IS EATING IN INFORMATIVE but its writing and cartoons are both witty and wise."
—Playboy

"EATING IN IS WELL ILLUSTRATED AND FUNNY. It isn't just a recipe book—it's also a book of strategy."
—People (Aus.)

"EATING IN IS FOR MEN WHO CHILL BEER, reheat coffee or dump garbage (in their kitchens.) It shows them how to make the transition from processed food to home-cooked romance."
—Miami Herald

"SLICE, DICE AND ENTICE might well be the subtitle. Prudes need not open the covers of this little gem of a cookbook."
—NJ News Tribune

"IT'S SIMPLY THE FUNNIEST COOKBOOK EVER WRITTEN . . . the ultimate tongue-in-cheek guide to better dating through cooking."
—The American Cooking Guild

EATING IN
The Official Single Man's Cookbook

*"Fills the gap between
Mrs. Paul and Julia Child."*

ALL RECIPES TESTED
GUARANTEED
EASY & IMPRESSIVE

ABOUT THE COOKS

RICH LIPPMAN used to boil fish sticks for dinner.
Now he cooks in every room of his house.

JOSÉ MALDONADO used to eat all his meals at the Y.
Now he's EATING IN.

JOE AZAR used to be a starving artist.
Now he draws women like mad.

OTHER BESTSELLERS
BY THE COOKS

Food on Beard—Table etiquette for the stubbled masses
The Endangered Moosewood Cookbook—Species extinction made easy
The Tin Palate Cookbook—Cooking for the hard-of-tasting
Fear of Frying—The quest for the zipless wok
Mastering the Art of French Tickling—101 uses for a baguette

TABLE OF CONTENTS

Chapter 3

continued . . .

Chapter 8

Chapter 10

Chapter 12

Appendix IV

Avoid the hazards of eating out.

CHAPTER 1

PRELUDE

Get Off On The Joy Of EATING IN.

"Behold the soft, dreamy gaze deep within a woman's eyes across a candlelit dinner table. As the seductive aroma of epicurean cuisine fills the air, and the euphoria from fine wine fills her head, you have before you a magnificent setting for romance, passion and pleasure."

— *Al Dente, Rome, 1923*

Everyone knows romance and dining go hand in hand. Taking your date to a fancy restaurant is one tasteful way to reach her heart. But now you can bring the same pleasures of eating out to your own home—and discover the quickest path to her heart is through your own kitchen.

Imagine the advantages:

You'll save big bucks on dinner, drinks and tips—not to mention parking, driving and embarrassing sobriety checkpoints.

You'll select the music and ambience of your liking, and enjoy romantic evenings cuddling in front of a roaring fire (or at least your Yulelog video).

You'll never have to deal with snail-paced service, haughty maitre d's, annoying rose peddlers or cigar-smoking loud-mouths.

And you'll side-step the big question, "Why don't we go back to my place?" because you'll already be there.

The Obvious Obstacle: Can You Cook?

EATING IN may sound like a terrific idea to you, but how will you ever impress your date if all you've ever made for dinner are reservations?

Will you simply jam leftover pizza slices into your toaster? Claim beef jerkies are packed with protein? Or try to convince her that Spam is in season this time of year?

Get a grip, buddy boy! Would a sane woman—or even a drunken floozy—let you cook dinner for her? Take this quiz and find out for yourself:

- ☐ Do you use your kitchen for anything more than chilling beer, stacking filthy dishes and raising blue-ribbon roaches?
- ☐ Would you be lost if Bird's Eye went blind? If the Green Giant got canned? If Charlie the Tuna finally got hooked?
- ☐ Has Mrs. Paul become like a mother to you? Is your idea of fine French cuisine a *Croissan'wich* at Burger King?
- ☐ Do you and your dog salivate together at the sound of your can opener? Is your ultimate fantasy a hot dinner date at Wendy's—*with Wendy?*

If you answered 'yes' to any one of these questions, you're undoubtedly suffering from the heartbreak of kitchen impotence. You couldn't get a meal up in the kitchen if you tried.

Why You (And Many Other Real Men) Can't Cook

Why are men with the potential to start World War III, explore the galaxies, and drink a fifth of Jack Daniels so stumped by a Julia Child recipe?

Back in your Dad's day, men didn't need to know how to cook. After a long hard day of engaging in manly pursuits, they could always count on a hot, hearty meal awaiting them at home.

Like it or not, fellas, those days have bit the dust.

Yet, as a child, odds are you were ordered "out of the kitchen till dinner's ready," thus preventing you from acquiring the many culinary secrets passed from mother to daughter.

This lack of basic kitchen know-how suddenly becomes a real problem when you first stand at the threshold of your own kitchen—alone, confused and hungry.

You know how to work a can opener, but not what to do with all those open cans. You're handy at fixing the pilot light, but can't tell boil from broil. And you're an expert at unclogging slop from the drain, but unwilling to make it into a sandwich.

And even your dog eats from a more varied menu, thanks to the chefs at Purina.

Faking It vs. Making It

You may think you can live on this lazy-man's diet forever, but one day you'll grow sick of it. One day you'll throw-up if you eat one more peanut butter and bologna roll-up. And one day you'll try to impress that special woman in your life by asking her over to your place for dinner.

"Good cooking's really not so tough," you think. "I'll just borrow one of Mom's beginner cookbooks and wing it."

But you soon learn that cooking even a simple dinner can be a real exercise in futility.

Why? Because most so-called "beginner" cookbooks presume you already own all the cookware. Stock the spices. Speak the lingo. Yearn to cook quiche. And have enough patience to follow a recipe that would confound Mr. Spock.

Look at the next two pages and see what we mean.

What Makes Simple Cooking So Difficult?

The hype on the cookbook jacket claims the recipes are easy. Why, then, are you instantly confused?

PORTUGUESE ROAST MOOSE LIPS WITH HOT UVULA STUFFING

A simply sinful meal that will have your friends licking your lips.

Ingredients

2 meaty moose lips (from matched set), debearded and deboned, with uvula reserved.

1 bouquet garni tied in cheesecloth with a pack of Certs (with Retsin)

1 imported fresh date

2 egg whites, beaten, for lip dredging

Cooked moose giblets, marinated overnight in author's Secret Dressing. See Vol. XII of author's cookbook for recipe.

½ cup clarified butter

1 fresh leek

4 potatoes in their jackets

2 lb. fish trimmings

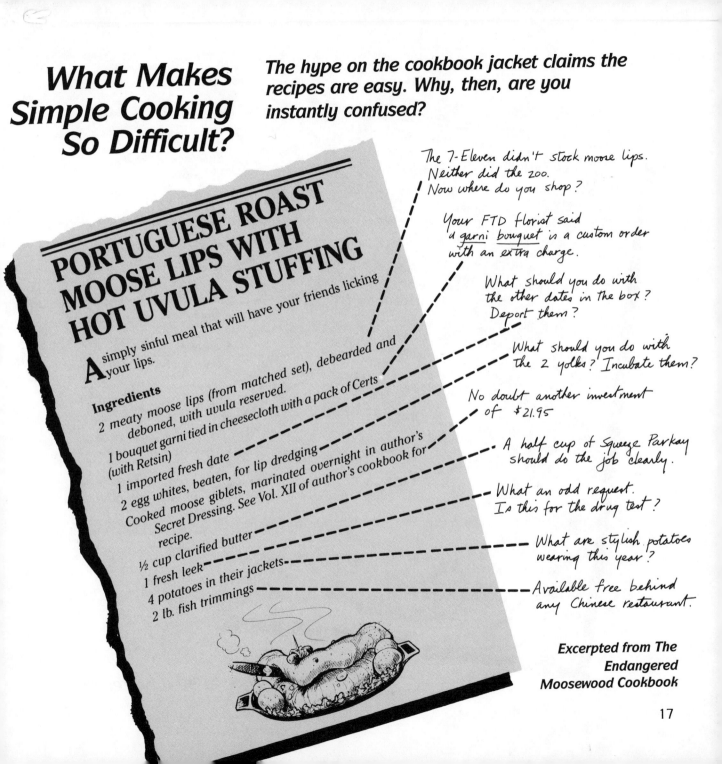

The 7-Eleven didn't stock moose lips. Neither did the zoo. Now where do you shop?

Your FTD florist said a garni bouquet is a custom order with an extra charge.

What should you do with the other dates in the box? Deport them?

What should you do with the 2 yolks? Incubate them?

No doubt another investment of $21.95

A half cup of Squeeze Parkay should do the job clearly.

What an odd request. Is this for the drug test?

What are stylish potatoes wearing this year?

Available free behind any Chinese restaurant.

Excerpted from The Endangered Moosewood Cookbook

17

PORTGUESE ROAST MOOSE LIPS WITH HOT UVULA STUFFING (continued)

Preparation

1. Turn moose lips into a colander.
2. Beat egg whites until stiff.
3. Sauté uvula until limp.
4. Push uvula inside lips to secure stuffing. Truss.
5. Slit date, remove pit and place nut in cavity. Wrap bacon around date.
6. Velvet the moose lips in clay moosting pan until lips are kissably soft. Prick moose lips well.
7. Repeat debearding with electrolysis. Rub with oil Celsius for 12 hours, or until moose talks.
8. Skewer moose lips tightly shut. Roast at 475° Celsius for 12 hours, or until moose talks.
9. Pucker moose lips into a grin and place on serving platter with lip drippings in a gravy boat.
10. Garnish with a fine Cuban cigar. Flambé at table. Serve with a fresh Geek Salad.

18 portions

Handwritten notes:

- You'll need a magician for this one.
- Does this mean the egg whites or you?
- This'll take all the fun out of cooking.
- No truss handy? How 'bout a jock?
- Sounds kinky — hope she's game.
- Available through their special catalog for only $199.99.
- Debeard, Oil + Prick? Sounds like a law firm.
- Will he ask for Rocky + his friends?
- At what pier is this gravy boat docked?
- How many other typos did the proofreader miss?
- You'll be eating mooselips sandwiches for months.

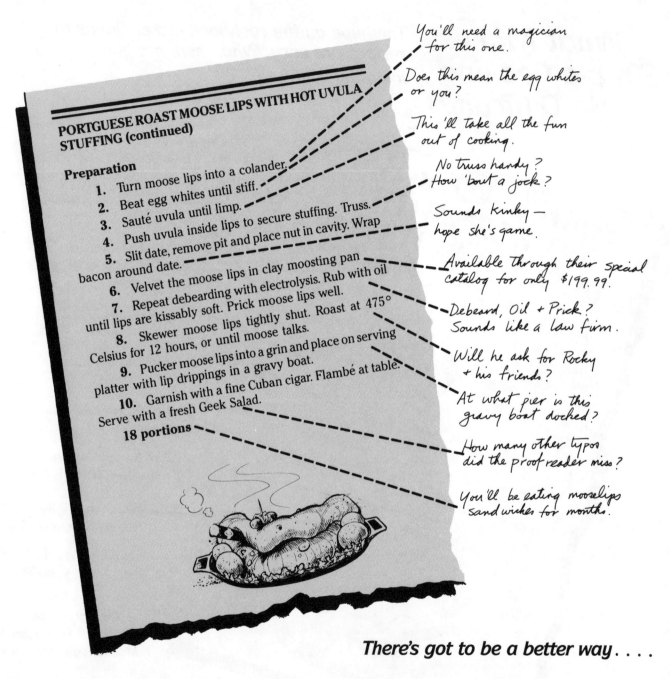

There's got to be a better way . . . .

TRY
EATING IN

And Experience Cooking in a New and Rewarding Way.

EATING IN was written for anyone who's fed up being a non-cook, by two single men who used to be non-cooks.

EATING IN does not assume you know any cooking basics.

EATING IN does not assume you want to spend endless hours slaving over a hot stove.

And EATING IN does not assume you own a blender, Cuisinart, microwave or salad spinner.

However, EATING IN does assume you want to learn how to prepare a few mouth-watering meals. And even impress a few mouth-watering women.

And who knows? You may start to hear your dinner dates remark, "You must have slaved all day in the kitchen for me," or "Why don't I prepare dinner for you next week," or "Your cooking is so good why don't we spend the rest of the night in a tangled embrace of sweaty passion."

Don't worry. You'll get used to it. We did.

EATING IN offers you all the knowledge you need to change your kitchen from wasteland to wonderland. It's the first user-friendly cookbook to unlock basic kitchen techniques never before revealed in one cookbook. Anywhere.

An average dinner date today can easily set you back $40–$60–even $80 and up. Now you can prepare an equivalent meal at home for less than one-third the cost.

You'll discover there are many more rewards from cooking than just great eating. You'll save tons of money, eat more balanced meals, explore more than the frozen food and beer aisles, and even learn how to buy wine.

But above all, you'll discover that women are truly impressed by a man who can cook. They're tired of doing all the slicing and dicing themselves, enjoy being served for a change, and genuinely appreciate your efforts. You'll even have fun!

In fact, an extensive nationwide survey recently revealed that today's single women overwhelmingly prefer men who can cook. Here are a few of their comments:

- *Pammi from Miami observed,* "Watching a man perform in the kitchen is very, very sexy."

- *Candy from Carlisle crooned,* "I can tell a lot about a bachelor by the way he wields his spatula . . . ."

- *Debbie of Dallas drawled,* "A man who can whip up a great dinner really impresses the pants off me."

- *Leeza of Los Angeles purred,* "I'm tired of eating out all the time and I want a guy who can really cook. In fact, I'm famished right now. Are you a survey-taker or the cook?"

So much for the benefits of taking your own surveys. Now on to the advantages of cooking your own meals.

21

CHAPTER 2

GEARING UP

Chuck that rusty Boy Scout mess kit. You're in the big leagues now.

One good place to start collecting kitchen gear is your mother's kitchen.

Are you well-equipped?

Hold your hyperbole. A spot-check around your kitchen will quickly reveal how you measure up:

- Does your laundry cup double as your measuring cup?
- Is your oven mitt autographed by Reggie Jackson?
- Did you buy your measuring spoons at a head shop?

Maybe these old stand-ins work when no one's watching, but imagine the horror on her face when she catches you basting her rump roast with a boot brush.

Get with it! Your goal is to turn her head—not her stomach.

Simply compare your own kitchen inventory to the illustrated EATING IN checklist of common-sense cookware. Then haul your butt to the nearest department store. You'll find all the equipment you need to prepare any recipe in this book.

And don't sweat about busting your budget. Because you're not purchasing a 250-bottle spice rack, solar vegetable steamer or Diesel Cuisinart. And you aren't investing in the entire Tupperware line or hosting their parties.

You're just getting down to basics.

So what are ya waiting for, Hairbag? Turn the page. 'Cause where gear's concerned, every girl's crazy 'bout a well-stocked man.

Common Sense Kitchen Gear

Y ou may be a whiz with a putty knife and a power drill, but don't use them to flip her chops or mix her martini. If you stock your kitchen with the basic gear shown here, you'll be able to cook any EATING IN recipe like a pro.

Two oven mitts*

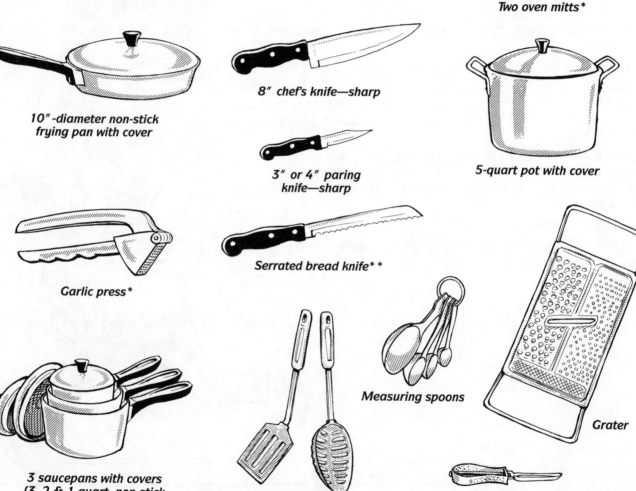

10"-diameter non-stick frying pan with cover

8" chef's knife—sharp

3" or 4" paring knife—sharp

5-quart pot with cover

Garlic press*

Serrated bread knife**

Measuring spoons

Grater

3 saucepans with covers (3, 2 & 1 quart, non-stick recommended)

Plastic spatula*

Slotted spoon*

Vegetable peeler

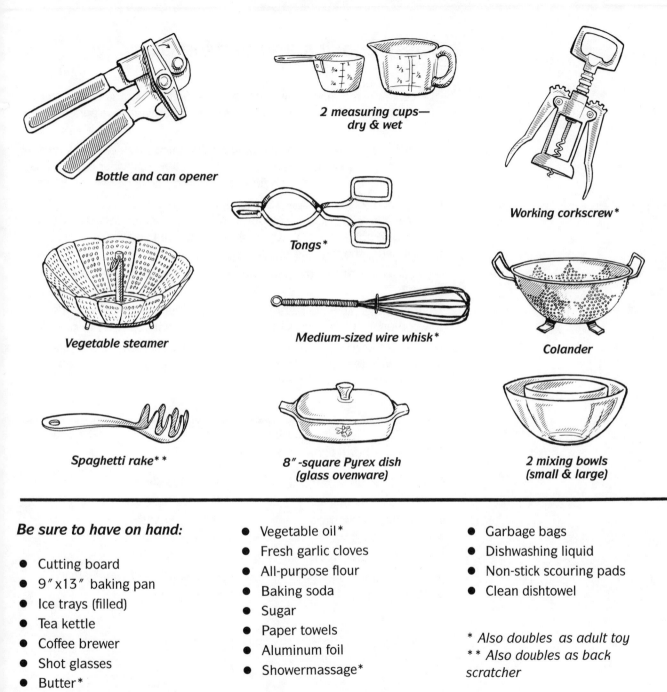

Bottle and can opener

**2 measuring cups—
dry & wet**

Working corkscrew*

Tongs*

Vegetable steamer

Medium-sized wire whisk*

Colander

Spaghetti rake**

**8" -square Pyrex dish
(glass ovenware)**

**2 mixing bowls
(small & large)**

Be sure to have on hand:

- Cutting board
- 9"x13" baking pan
- Ice trays (filled)
- Tea kettle
- Coffee brewer
- Shot glasses
- Butter*

- Vegetable oil*
- Fresh garlic cloves
- All-purpose flour
- Baking soda
- Sugar
- Paper towels
- Aluminum foil
- Showermassage*

- Garbage bags
- Dishwashing liquid
- Non-stick scouring pads
- Clean dishtowel

* Also doubles as adult toy
*** Also doubles as back
scratcher*

Classy Cooking and Serving Gear

You've set the mood. The lights are low. Soft music drifts from your stereo. And the moment arrives to tempt her with your perfectly-prepared dinner.

Tenderly you seat her at the dinner table and await her reaction to the grand setting before her: mismatched plastic utensils, divider paper plates, leftover Slurpee cups and a blazing Chanukah candelabra—set on Sunday funnies placemats.

Now you're puzzled. Is she doubled-over in laughter because of your meager attempt at social graces? Or is she just reading the Peanuts cartoon under the tiny packets of carry-out ketchup?

Saaay. . . isn't this the point where the camera pans over to Rod Serling?

Remember, cooking tasty food is only one half of a successful meal. How you present the food is the other vital element you need to consider.

You can keep your dinner out of the Twilight Zone and add a touch of class to your evening with these basic serving items. And you'll never have to face a dinner alone with Rod.

Make sure your table is set with:

- Matching silverware
- Matching dishes
- Matching glassware
- Clean tablecloth
- Matching placemats
- Matching cloth napkins
- Wine glasses
- Wine cooler
- Butter dish
- Serving dishes
- Flower vase
- Salt and pepper mills
- Bread basket
- Candles and candlesticks
- Sugar bowl

A perfect place setting for the perfect place.

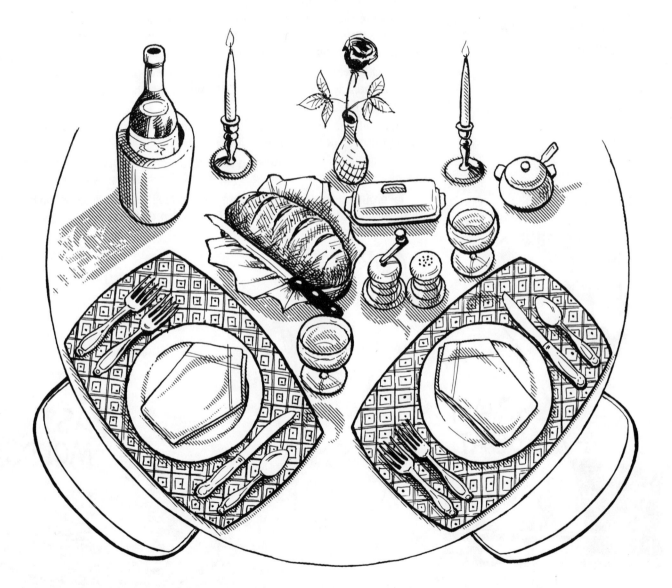

Wimpy Kitchen Widgets

Don't ever let her catch you using any of these.

Some cooking concepts will forever remain a mystery to single men. Like who really orders those ridiculous kitchen gadgets hawked incessantly on late-night TV?

Despite the announcer's miracle claims, these gadgets are guaranteed to do only three things: jam up your kitchen drawers, melt down in your dishwasher and cast doubt on your manhood.

Consider yourself forewarned! How will you explain to your date why you're sheepishly reaching for the "Jar Aid" when she asks you to unscrew the mustard?

How will she react when she catches you gaily scooping away with a "melon baller?" (Real men don't ball melons.)

Or will she wonder why you'd want to use a hamburger press to shape your meat?

Take our advice. Stifle the temptation to buy these ridiculous kitchen contraptions lest your date fear you'll soon turn them on her.

GRAVY BOAT

FAT GRAVY

CORN STRIPPER

PASTRY MOLDS

DOUBLE MELON BALLER

CHEESE PLANE

THE AMAZING GORBACHEF ™

WITH GLASNOST ATTACHMENTS

29

CHAPTER 3

THE INVITATION

Be sure you check your guest's dietary preferences in advance.

Can you name several foods you're sure your dinner guest enjoys? If you can't, you run the awful risk of serving her a dish she'll feed to your potted palm.

Unlike eating out, where she can select meals from a menu, in your home she's obliged to eat what you place in front of her. Or at least pick at the breaded coating.

This unfortunate oversight can lead to awkward situations.

For instance, what if you proudly serve her a juicy filet mignon only to have her proclaim, "Since when do vegetarians eat poor defenseless animals with big brown eyes?"

How would you respond if she shrieks, "I'd rather be whipped than eat brussels sprouts." (*Hint:* quickly determine whether this is pure revulsion or an urgent request.)

Or how would you explain to the emergency room doctors that *your* cooking triggered her fatal allergic reaction?

You can avoid these awkward moments by planning your menu with her in advance. When you set the date, just say, "How does one of my famous chicken specialties sound to you?"

When she responds, *"Mmmmmmmmmm.* Chicken sounds fabulous," that's your cue to locate a chicken recipe in this book. Read how to cook it. And get plucking.

Your date's not the main course. Try not to make her feel like she is.

A proper dinner invitation can mean the difference between a perfectly-planned evening and a disaster after dark. The invitation is your chance-in-advance to arouse your date's taste buds—not her survival instincts.

Just imagine how she'll feel arriving at your place for dinner. At night. Alone. Unarmed. Fretting that the date muffins you're planning to devour are hers. That the suckling pig will not be her dinner but her host. And that dessert will be nothing more than a chilled Reddi-Whip surprise.

Do your best to help her feel at home. If she's eyeing the exits, pour her a glass of wine. Serve your appetizers. Romance her with your newfound culinary skills. And prepare her for the feast of her dreams.

Remember, even though you have the home court advantage, that's no excuse to take advantage. Act like a gracious host and you'll guarantee she'll be back for more. Act like a perfect ass and you'll be kissing hers good-bye.

Just imagine how she'll feel arriving at your place for dinner. At night. Alone. Unarmed.

CHAPTER 4

CLEANING FOR SUCCESS

You may not even notice that nauseating house-wide odor anymore. But rest assured she will never forget.

It's a bit late to begin cleaning when your dinner guest is ringing your doorbell. And if the squalor in your place makes her run for her life, your next guest may be from the Department of Health.

What's the solution? Either pray for the White Tornado to touch down, or slip the health inspector a crisp fifty.

Wait! You've overlooked your third—and best—option.

Cleaning.

It's the same thing your mother always nagged you to do and you never did. But now you're going to do it for a better reward than your mother could ever give you.

Housecleaning means a lot more than simply shoving all your girlie magazines under the couch. It requires planning, motivation, time and lots of coffee to do the job right.

Don't wait until the last minute, or you may wind up using your one clean pillow case for a vacuum cleaner bag. Your hair brush to scrub the bathroom bowl. Or your Speed Stick as an air freshener.

Take a tip from the Boy Scouts. *Be prepared.* Pry those flip tops and bottle caps out of the rug. Sweep the Cheerios under the refrigerator. And announce check-out time at Ye Olde Roache Inne.

But that's just the beginning. Break out the Hefty bags and rev up the vacuum. You've got a lot of work to do—and not much time. The Main Event is just around the corner. . . .

Don't use masking tape to pick up lint and crumbs from the carpet. Borrow a vacuum cleaner. Or spray the cat with Endust and turn her loose.

Your Chaotic Kitchen

A clean, well-organized kitchen will do more than make your cooking easier. It also leads your dinner guest to believe you are preparing a sanitary meal for her.

Take an objective look around your kitchen:

- Is the inside of your oven window coated with Shake 'n' Bake?
- When your refrigerator starts to smell like a sewer, do you merely stir the baking soda?
- Do the stains on your garbage pail match the stains on the wall behind it? On the floor below it? On the ceiling above it?

You can count on your guest giving your kitchen the white glove test before allowing anything you prepare there to pass her lips. And heaven help you if her finger comes up grimy.

Imagine how she'll recoil in horror if she catches you shaking out the toaster to bread her pork chops. Sees that the baking pans on your shelf are already greased. Or smells dinner burning when all you're doing is making tea.

The kitchen should be your first stop on your cleaning circuit. You'll not only strip away years of grease and grime, but also reveal the room's original colors.

Remember, your kitchen should look and smell like a place where you want to prepare food. Not regurgitate it.

Your Lurid Living and Dining Rooms

While you're in the kitchen busily preparing dinner, your guest will be seated in the living room hungrily awaiting your feast. So it's a bright idea to clean your living room in advance to avoid spoiling her appetite.

To clear away the Animal House effect, be sure to sweep out the cigarette butts, pizza crusts and dirty socks collecting under the sofa cushions.

Don't use masking tape to pick up lint, crumbs and seeds from the carpet. Borrow a vacuum cleaner. Or spray the cat with Endust and turn her loose.

Clean your toenail clippings out of the ash tray. Get your hospital test results off the coffee table. And don't leave your credit card statements out for her amusement.

Well before you move the party into your dining room, wipe the dinner table of crumbs, jelly, syrup, candle wax, sugar grit and stuck bugs. Flip the placemats once. And as a nice touch, place a fresh-cut rose in a bud vase. Not a Bud can.

Throw out the mountains of old newspapers piling up on the chairs. Toss out all the old beer bottles and cans before she thinks you're running a recycling center. Hang up all shirts, ties and shorts draped over lamps and doorknobs.

And when you're all done, be sure to ask an honest friend to come over to your place and smell it for you.

Man Cannot Live On Beer Alone.

Your Toxic Bathroom

Even if you beg her not to go, your date is going to have to use your bathroom. So why risk ending a perfectly romantic evening simply because your bathroom reeks like the gorilla house at the zoo?

The truth is, you may have stopped smelling this putrid odor years ago, but rest assured—your date will never forget it.

Step boldly into your bathroom and look around:

- Has your bathtub become a blooming landscape of mold, mildew and mushrooms?
- Is your only face towel still damp from Rover's annual bath?
- Does the Pentagon want to deploy your shower curtain for biological warfare?

Remember, spending just two hurried minutes in your bathroom could be an odoriferous nightmare for her. Especially if you can't recall the last time you cleaned it.

Make sure you scrub the sink, toilet, shower, floor and mirrors. A blow torch performs this task admirably and kills germs on contact.

Don't forget to get a fresh supply of toilet paper, soap, clean towels, tissues, toothpaste, mouthwash, dental floss, air freshener and Alka-Seltzer (just in case).

Remove all recognizable hairs clinging to the soap. Spoon out the scuzz from the soap dish. Rinse out your garbage pail. Sweep out the fur from behind the door. Flush the toilet.

And if you're really out to impress her, wipe the dew drops off the toilet seat and shift it to the down position.

Your Disheveled Bedroom

Your dinner guest may have absolutely no intention of ever setting foot into your bedroom. But in the event she's feeling a little footloose, you'll sorely regret not having cleaned up ahead of time.

Imagine how fast her romantic mood will disappear when she spies earrings that aren't hers. Lacy undergarments that certainly aren't yours. And battery-operated devices she can't figure out.

Get with it, Romeo. One quick glance around your unkempt bedroom and the only thing she'll beat that night is a hasty retreat.

Do you have a year's worth of dirty laundry growing in the corner? Is the floor sprinkled with sand from last summer's beach trip? Does your pillow case resemble a used dental bib? Are the patterns on your sheets not the ones designed by the manufacturer?

Don't expose yourself to unnecessary risks. Change your sheets. Make your bed. Vacuum your floor. Windex the mirrors on your ceiling. Inventory your protection. And be sure to load a fresh roll of videotape in your SkyCam.

Quiz

Get out your No. 2 pencils and test your hospitality quotient by answering these probing lifestyle questions. Circle your answers True or False and rate yourself with the scoring key below.

T or F Women appreciate men who maintain clean and orderly homes.

T or F Women feel comfortable in your home when you behave in a courteous and gentlemanly manner.

T or F Women are glad to pick up last-minute dinner items on their way over.

T or F Women appreciate it when you belch show tunes at the dinner table.

T or F Women are eager to cut your meat into bite-sized pieces and feed them to you.

T or F Women beg to wash your dishes while you watch football and guzzle beer.

T or F Women consider thorough flossing between each course good oral hygiene.

T or F Women love to hear you spin lewd tales about your past conquests.

T or F Women will thank you when you leave the toilet seat up in the middle of the night.

T or T Women will mock your manners in front of your family and friends and on 60 Minutes if you fail this quiz.

Bachelor Scoring Key

All 10 correct Sounds like you're already EATING IN.

9 correct High EATING IN potential. Don't ask her to belch in harmony, though.

1-8 correct You're worthless and weak. Stay a virgin or go herd sheep. Or send $13.95 for answer key and study guide to: EATS, Princeton, NJ.

Appeteasers

Machos	51	Broiled Mushrooms Parmesan	52
Cheese 'n' Cracker Platter	51	Eat It Raw Vegetable Platter	52
Magic Mushrooms	52	Amazing Shortcut Soup	52
		Before Dinner Cocktails	53-54

Entrees

Poultry

Dijon Chicken
Tender chicken broiled and basted in a
tangy mustard-garlic sauce. 58

Chicken Marsala
Boneless breasts pan-fried to perfection in
Marsala wine and topped with melted
Parmesan cheese. 74

Hen House Rock
Fresh Rock Cornish game hens packed full
of tasty walnut-raisin stuffing and baked to a
juicy finish. 70

Tasty Breasts Sesame
Boneless chicken pan-fried in a zesty herb
dressing mixed with fresh lime juice and
topped with sesame seeds. 64

Beef

Orange Steak Sunrise
Tempting T-Bones broiled to your liking in
a tangy orange sauce. Unique! 66

Steak (*Her Name Here*)
Delicious Delmonicos pan-fried in a savory
steak sauce and served flambé. 78

Sonny's Secret Spaghetti Sauce
Homemade spaghetti sauce brimming with
green peppers, onions, mushrooms, garlic
and ground beef, served on your favorite
pasta. 76

Pork

Thick-Cut Pork Chops
Tasty pork chops seared quickly in olive oil,
garlic and basil and then pan-fried to a
golden brown. 62

Seafood

Shrimp Scampi
Fresh butterfly shrimp pan-fried in savory garlic-butter sauce spooned over white rice and served with warm French bread.   68

Savory Salmon with Creamy Cucumber Sauce
Fresh salmon fillets poached and then topped with mouth-watering cucumber sauce and sprinkled with dill weed.   72

Opening Night Flounder*
Fresh flounder pan-fried in olive oil and topped with sautéed mushrooms, onions and garlic. Less filling! Tastes great!   80
* *Lite 'n' Tite*

Vegetarian

Fettuccini Alfredo
Fresh fettuccini noodles coated with Alfredo's rich, creamy sauce.   60

Hot Hawaiian Luau*
Fresh vegetables quickly stir-fried with chunks of juicy pineapple, ginger and garlic and served on a hot bed of rice.
* *Lite 'n' Tite*   82

A Little on the Side

Ginger Carrots	87	Zesty Garlic Bread	89
New Potatoes Parmesan	86	Hot Buttered Beer Bread	89
Mini Orange Carrots	86	Cheese 'n' Butter Linguine	91
Broc Around the Clock	87	Miami Rice	91
Stir-Fried Garlic Green Beans	88	Rice 'n' Shrooms	91
Twice-Baked Spuds	88		

Salads

EATING IN Salad	90	Spinach Salad	90
		Who Made the Salad? Salad	90

Designer Butters

Honey Butter	91	Garlic Butter	91

Desserts

Chef Tell's Favorite	93	Chocolate Pear Cups	94
Peaches Pistachio	94	Hot Vermont Weekend	95
Berry Berry Good Amaretto	94	Kahlua Volcano	95
Chocolate-Dipped Strawberries	94		

Afterglow

Fresh Fruit Bowl	97	Chocolate Truffles	97
Strawberries in Champagne	97	Cordials	97

Breakfast Drinks & Eye-Openers

Everything from fresh-squeezed Screwdrivers to piping hot coffee concoctions. 100-101

Breakfasts

Scrambled Eggs Imperial	102	*Side Orders*	
The Morning After Pancake	104	Homemade Hash Browns	110
French Toast a l'Orange	106	Fresh Fruit Bowl	110
Eggs Mc(*Your Name Here*)	108	Bakin' Bacon	111
		Cinnamon Toast	111
		English Muffins	111

& Pronunciation Guide

White Wines

Chablis	sha-bleé
Chenin Blanc	sheh-nan blahnk
Fumé Blanc	fu-may´ blahnk
Kabinett	kab-in-et´
Moselle	moe-zell´
Piesporter	peas´-porter
Pinot Chardonnay	peá-no shar-doh-nay´
Pinot Blanc	peá-no blahnk
Pinot Grigio	peá-no greé-zho
Pouilly-Fumé	poo-yee fu-may´
Pouilly-Fuissé	poo-yee fwee-say´
Rhine	rine
Riesling	reez´-ling
Sauterne	saw-turn´
Sauvignon Blanc	so-vee-nyonh-blahnk
JAP Whine	tayk-mee-too-my-aaaaah´-mee

Red Wines

Beaujolais	boh-zho-lay´
Bordeaux	bor-doe´
Cabernet Sauvignon	kab-er-nay´ so-vee-nyonh´
Chianti	key-yon´-tee
Côtes du Rhône	koat-doo-roan
Pinot Noir	peé-no nwar
Rioja	ree-oh´-ha
Rosé	ro-zay´
Zinfandel	zin-fahn-dell´
Mad Dog 20/20	mad´-dawg twen´-tee twen´-tee

CHAPTER 6

POPPING THE CORK

An Easy Guide To Selecting and Serving The Correct Wine.

Dashing into a liquor store and grabbing any old bottle of wine is like randomly selecting an album in a record store. It's dumb.

But what should you do if you don't know wine from Woolite? Trust some spaced-out stockboy's recommendation? Search for the fanciest label? Or ask the oenophiles gathered in the back alley what they're drinking?

You can turn wine buying into a rewarding and enjoyable experience by following these simple guidelines:

- *Serve white wine with fish and poultry; red wine with red meat.* Usually. There are some exceptions, such as serving certain reds with salmon, certain whites with veal, and Blue Nun with certain priests.

- *Match the intensity of the wine to the intensity of the food.* Create a balance. Serve a light, mildly flavored wine with a light, mildly flavored dish. Choose a savory, intensely flavored wine to accompany a dish of the same description. Ripple, for instance, goes down well with burgers in a bag.

- *You'll be extremely satisfied with wine costing between $6 and $16.* Spend more if you desire a prestigious or rare label. Spend less if you want to speed up your digestive process.

- *Serve no wine before it's time.* Before breakfast, for instance (unless, of course, it's chilled and sparkling).

Every main course in this book includes an appropriate wine suggestion. However, it's up to you to select the vintner, vintage, grape and price. This can still be a difficult task, unless you enlist the help of a local wine merchant. If he's knowledgeable, sober and speaks English, he should be able to recommend the best wine for your money and your meal.

Remember, the difference between the cost of buying your own wine—and ordering it at a restaurant—can be enough to pay for the entire meal you're cooking.

To chill or not to chill?

Always chill white wines, blushes (rosés) and champagnes (45°-50°). In a time crunch, it's tacky to quick-chill wine on the rocks. Simply place the bottle in your freezer for no more than a half-hour (any longer and you'll be serving Chablis-Slurpees or Pouilly-Popsicles).

Serve red wines at room temperature (60°-70°). Be sure to uncork red wine at least a half-hour in advance so it can breathe. (You too should uncork in advance so she can breathe.)

Screw the cork. Not yourself.

Although there are many different devices available to open wine, all you need is a basic corkscrew you can operate with skill, safety and style.

Stifle the temptation to buy overpriced "executive cork pullers." Ignore those late-night TV offers for NASA-tested hydraulic corkwood extractors. And never buy wines with screw-caps (unless you plan to pour them from brown paper bags).

To open the bottle, simply cut away the foil and wipe the top clean. Insert the corkscrew and let 'er rip. If it rips too much, remember that shredded cork doesn't spoil wine. Neither does pushing the cork down into the bottle. Just be on guard for comments like, "This is the first wine I've ever had to chew," or "Did you pay any extra for the cork bits?"

If your wine contains sediment, it should be decanted. Pour it slowly into a broad-mouth decanter, and stop pouring just before you get to the sediment. Swig it when she's not looking.

Pouring and serving with style.

Your wine glasses should be large enough to contain a generous serving when they are about half full. You may be fond of your Yoplait container collection, but stick with traditional wine glasses. The wine will taste better.

When it's time to serve the wine, pour yourself a small amount and savor the bouquet. Swirl it over your palate. If it's good, pour your date a glassful and then pour one for yourself. If it's bad simply exclaim, "Damn! Imagine spending $50 for a bottle of bad wine."

CHAPTER 7

FOREPLAY

Tempting drinks and appeteasers to whet your woman's passionate palate. Just don't forget about dinner.

Get your evening off to a good start and set the stage for a great meal to come. These appeteasers are less filling—and they taste great. You can prepare them in advance and match them to complement your main dish. You'll then be free to relax with your date and really start cooking.

Machos

1 small bag regular tortilla cheeps (not nacho or cheese-flavored)
● *4 oz. Monterey Jack cheese* ● *small jar sliced jalapeño peppers*
● *3 scallions* ● *½ cup sour cream.*

Heep cheeps into pile in baking pan. Grate cheese over cheeps and add jalapeños to taste. Broil for 3 minutes or until you have a cheese melt-down. Meanwhile, cut scallions (page 135). Transfer Machos to serving platter and sprinkle with chopped scallions. Serve with sour cream in a clean bowl.

Cheese 'n' Cracker Platter

Always a hit, unless you serve gooey processed cheese spread. Try any of these instead: Camembert, Gouda, Gruyere, Jarlsberg, Baby Swiss, Edam, Sharp Cheddar—plus pepperoni slices ● *crackers or French bread or slices of fresh fruit.*

Unwrap the cheeses and let them come to room temperature before serving. Cut away any paper and wax and arrange on a platter next to a cheese knife. If you're serving fruit, cut into bite-sized pieces no more than a few minutes before serving.

Magic Mushrooms

10 bite-sized fresh mushrooms ● a small bottle of your favorite vinaigrette or Italian dressing ● small container of grated Parmesan cheese.

Wipe mushrooms clean with damp cloth and put in bowl. Pour dressing over mushrooms until submerged and add 1 Tb. grated Parmesan cheese. Mix together, cover bowl and refrigerate 2 hours or overnight. When ready to serve, drain off dressing, transfer mushrooms to serving platter and eat with toothpicks. Keep napkins handy.

Broiled Mushrooms Parmesan

10 medium-sized fresh mushrooms ● small container grated Parmesan cheese ● 2 Tb. butter ● seasoned salt.

Wipe mushrooms clean with damp cloth. Pull stems out completely from caps. Place caps upside down on foil-lined baking pan (or use pan in toaster oven). Chop stems finely and stuff into caps. Dot with slivers of butter and sprinkle with grated Parmesan cheese and seasoned salt. Broil for 3 minutes or until tops are lightly browned.

Eat It Raw

Your choice of what's in season: carrot sticks ● cauliflowerets ● celery sticks ● broccoli florets ● cherry tomatoes ● sliced fresh mushrooms ● sliced cucumbers ● sliced green and red peppers.

Rinse and cut up a small quantity of two or three vegetables listed above and put on serving platter (a visit to a supermarket salad bar will save you time). Buy a zesty dip and pour it into a small serving bowl.

Amazing Shortcut Soup

Your favorite brand of premium canned soup.

Throw away soup can before your guest arrives. Heat soup and serve. Garnish with parsley sprigs (fresh so they'll float), a dash of sherry and herbed croutons. Accompany with crackers. If she asks for the recipe, change the subject to shoes.

Before Dinner Cocktails

Loosen up, Sandy baby! Here's your chance to get your evening going strong. Serve your favorite cocktail or pop open the wine before you slide dinner into the oven. Just don't forget you invited her over for dinner, too!

Here are a few tasty classics that work for us:

Bloody Mary

1 oz. vodka ● 3 oz. tomato juice ● 1 Tb. lemon juice ● dash Worcestershire sauce ● dash Tabasco sauce ● pepper to taste.

Combine ingredients. Shake. Pour over ice into rocks glass. Garnish with celery stick or lemon slice. (Hint: prepare mix in advance and chill. Add vodka when ready to serve.)

Black Russian

2 oz. vodka ● 1 oz. Kahlua.

Combine ingredients. Shake. Pour over ice into rocks glass.

Between The Sheets

1 oz. rum ● 1 oz. brandy ● 1 oz. Cointreau ● ½ oz. lemon juice.

Combine ingredients. Shake. Pour over ice into rocks glass.

Cape Codder

1 oz. vodka ● 3 oz. cranberry juice.

Combine ingredients. Stir. Pour over ice into rocks glass.

Whiskey Sour

2 oz. whiskey ● 2 Tb. lemon juice ● ½ tsp. powdered sugar.

Combine ingredients. Shake vigorously. Pour over ice into rocks glass. Garnish with orange or lemon slice and maraschino cherry.

Daiquiri

2 oz. light rum ● *1½ Tb. lime juice* ● *½ tsp. powdered sugar.*

Combine ingredients. Shake. Pour over ice into cocktail glass.

Tequila Sunrise

2 oz. tequila ● *1 tsp. grenadine* ● *4 oz. orange juice.*

Combine tequila and orange juice. Shake. Pour over ice into rocks glass. Pour in grenadine slowly.

Mocktails

For drinks without the alcohol or hangover.

Virgin Mary

Same as Bloody Mary, but leave out the vodka.

Randy Andy

½ glass orange juice ● *½ glass grapefruit juice* ● *1 orange slice.*

Combine and shake. Pour over ice into rocks glass. Garnish with orange slice.

Wet Willie

2 oz. cranberry juice ● *1 oz. orange juice* ● *½ oz. lemon juice* ● *ginger ale to top off.*

Mix ingredients over ice into 6 oz. rocks glass and top off with ginger ale. Garnish with orange slice.

STOP!

**Be sure to closely
examine the entire
appendix
(on pages 125-137)
before you start
cooking.**

Dinner is served!

CHAPTER 8

THE MAIN EVENT

As the first bite melts in her mouth, she'll know she's on to something hot.

This is the magic moment she's been waiting for. She's finally unearthed a man who can effortlessly whip up a gourmet feast for her. And who isn't married.

It's *your* moment of truth, too. Your chance to deliver everything you've been promising—a sumptuous dinner that's well-planned, well-prepared—and looks great.

Observe, as the aroma from your cooking starts to work its magic. She'll become hungry with anticipation. Her taste buds will tingle. Her stomach will purr. And if you've followed the advice in this book, you'll surge with confidence. Not incontinence.

Just use these time-saving techniques to make your last hectic minutes a lot easier. That way you'll look like a winner—not a beginner.

Be sure to read and follow the Power Shopping Guide at the beginning of each recipe before you pick up your ingredients. It's designed to help you speed through the grocery store (because you're probably behind schedule already).

Prepare your workspace and assemble your ingredients before your guest arrives. Read through the entire recipe twice. Pre-measure, pre-slice and pre-mix whenever possible.

Always begin with the items that take the longest time to cook. Don't forget to keep track of cooking times. Watch out for foods boiling over, burning up or drying out. Be sure to refresh her drink often. And when you're finished cooking, turn off all appliances, dim the lights and pour the wine.

Arrange your dinner artistically on the plates—don't pile it on mess-hall style. Use side dishes if the main plates look too crowded. Toss on a garnish, such as a sprig of parsley or a wedge of lemon, for some color. Remember, the more appetizing your dinner looks, the better you'll look. And isn't that the whole point?

Good luck! Bon appetit! And be sure to drop us a line and tell us how good it was for you.

DIJON CHICKEN

The easiest chick in the book.

Preparation Time
6 minutes

Cooking Time
25 minutes

Equipment Checklist
Small mixing bowl, tongs,
broiler pan, aluminum foil

Power Shopping Guide
Meat: 1 fresh whole pre-cut
chicken
Produce: 3 garlic cloves,
6 scallions
Condiment: 8 oz. jar tangy
Dijon mustard
Seasoning: pepper

Serves 2

Empty stove of all items you've stashed there.

Remove broiler pan with tray and line the tray with aluminum foil. Slide back into broiler 4"-6" below heat source. Set oven to broil.

With oven mitt, partially slide out hot broiler pan and add chicken, skin-side down. Broil 7 minutes, then shift parts around with tongs for even cooking. Broil 7 more minutes.

Flip chicken and broil 5 more minutes. Smear tops with mustard mixture and broil another 3-5 minutes. When you cut into thickest piece and meat is white and juices are no longer red, it's time to eat!

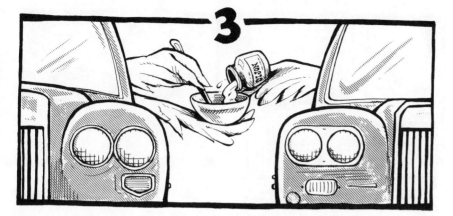

Spoon 4 Tb. Dijon mustard into small bowl. Mince 3 cloves garlic, cut up 6 scallions (page 135) and mix in the bowl.

Thoroughly rinse chicken, pat dry and sprinkle lightly with pepper (just the parts you plan to eat—not the weird backs, necks and innards).

After pan has cooled, be sure to peel off slimy aluminum foil. If you forget, be prepared for an attack of mustard gas within 48 hours. . . .

GOOD
Serve with Stir-Fried Garlic Green Beans (page 88).

BETTER
Serve with Garlic Italian Bread (page 89).

BEST
Serve Listerine and breath mints for dessert.

FROM THE VINEYARD
Sauvignon Blanc or Pouilly Fumé. With strong Dijon, try a full-bodied Beaujolais.

FETTUCCINI ALFREDO

If you can boil water, you too can cook like Alfredo.

Preparation Time
10 minutes

Cooking Time
10 minutes (after water boils)

Equipment Checklist
Large pot, 10″ non-stick frying pan, colander, two forks

Power Shopping Guide
Pasta: 16 oz. package fettuccini noodles
Dairy: 8 oz. canister grated Parmesan cheese, 1 stick sweet butter (not margarine), ½ pint heavy (whipping) cream
Lube: vegetable oil
Seasoning: ground white pepper, salt

. Serves 2

Fill a large pot ⅔ full with water. Add 1 Tb. salt and 1 Tb. vegetable oil and bring to rolling boil over high heat. (*Hint:* Use stove.)

Reduce heat to medium and *carefully* drop 2 portions of fettuccini (about ⅓ of the box) into boiling water. Stir. Follow directions on package for *al dente* cooking time.

With your oven mitts, drain fettuccini into colander. Shake off excess water. (*Hint:* Do it over the sink.)

Return frying pan to burner at low heat. Add noodles to sauce and sprinkle with 3 oz. of grated cheese. Toss with two large forks until cheese melts.

Five minutes before fettuccini is ready, in frying pan melt 6 Tb. butter at low heat. Don't let it sizzle!

Add 4 Tb. heavy cream to melted butter, increase to medium heat and stir until slightly thickened and bubbly. Then remove from heat.

Fettuccini is ready when one strand sticks to wall or tastes the way you like it. Save some for dinner.

Add another 3 oz. of cheese, sprinkle lightly with white pepper and toss again. Immediately divide noodles between two dinner plates and top each with 1 oz. of grated cheese.

GOOD
Serve with your choice of dinner salads (page 90).

BETTER
Try fresh fettuccini noodles available free from sympathetic friends with pasta machines.

BEST
For a taste Alfredo would call his own, grate 8 oz. of *parmigiano reggiano* cheese—the *real* imported Parmesan.

FROM THE VINEYARD
A full-bodied California chardonnay or chianti classico

THICK-CUT PORK CHOPS

You'll lick your chops, not bust them, with these squealin' beauties.

Preparation Time
2 minutes

Cooking Time
14 minutes

Equipment Checklist
10″ non-stick frying pan, tongs

Power Shopping Guide
Meat: four 1¼″-thick pork chops
Lube: olive oil
Produce: 1 garlic clove
Seasoning: dried basil, pepper

Serves 2

Grocery store butchers often cut pork chops too thin.

Yell at butcher to cut four 1¼″-thick pork chops for you and to trim the fat.

While oil is still hot, carefully add chops. Sprinkle lightly with pepper and ½ tsp. basil. Sear (brown) chops, flip them over to sear on other side, and sprinkle again with pepper and ½ tsp. basil.

Lower heat to medium and cook another 6 minutes. Flip again and cook till done (when no pink remains inside—about 6-10 minutes). Remove from heat.

Politely.

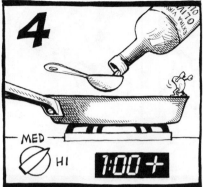

When you're safely home, lightly crush 1 garlic clove with the side of a knife and remove papery skin. Coat frying pan with 2 Tb. olive oil and heat at medium-high. Add garlic and stir 1-2 minutes until it's tanned (not burned).

Remove garlic with spoon.

Serve politely.

GOOD
Serve with Broc Around the Clock (page 87).

BETTER
Serve with heated apple sauce topped with cinnamon.

BEST
Find a new butcher.

FROM THE VINEYARD
Beaujolais or Tavel Rosé

*T*ASTY BREASTS SESAME

You've tried the rest, now try the breast.

Preparation Time
4 minutes

Cooking Time
5 minutes

Equipment Checklist
10″ non-stick frying pan with cover, tongs, paring knife

Power Shopping Guide
Meat: 4 fresh boneless chicken breast halves
Produce: 1 fresh lime, 1 garlic clove
Dressing: 1 small bottle of your favorite Italian salad dressing
Seasoning: sesame seeds, pepper

Serves 2

Pour Italian dressing into frying pan to ¼′ depth. Mince 1 garlic clove (page 135) and add to dressing. Heat at medium-low setting.

Ooops! Sorry. . .we meant ¼ *inch* depth.

Cut half the lime into 4 slices.

Cap each breast with one lime slice, then squeeze juice from remaining lime half over breasts. Cover for 4 minutes. Dinner's ready when inside of thickest breast is all white.

Rinse breasts in water and remove any skin. When dressing is hot, arrange breasts in single layer in the frying pan.

Sprinkle lightly with pepper and sesame seeds. (*Hint:* it's easier to buy the seeds than to pick them off hamburger buns.)

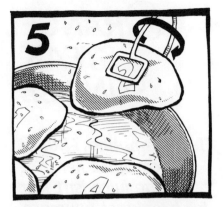

Turn breasts over when they turn white on frying side (1-2 minutes). Sprinkle with a few more sesame seeds.

Remove top from breasts. Admire and eat.

GOOD
Serve with Broc Around the Clock (page 87).

BETTER
Spoon sauce over a bed of hot pasta and top with breasts.

BEST
Serve on a bed of hot spinach linguine.

FROM THE VINEYARD
Sauvignon Blanc or Pinot Grigio

ORANGE STEAK SUNRISE

These tempting T-Bones will convince her that orange juice isn't just for breakfast anymore.

Preparation Time
5 minutes

Cooking Time
10 minutes (for medium-rare)

Equipment Checklist
Broiler pan, small mixing bowl, grater, tongs, aluminum foil, knife

Power Shopping Guide
Meat: two 8-10 oz. T-Bone steaks or one 16 oz. Porterhouse steak
Produce: 1 fresh orange
Lube: vegetable oil
Seasoning: chili powder, salt, pepper

Serves 2

Rinse orange. *Carefully* grate 1 Tb. peel from around outside of orange. Cut orange in half and set aside.

In mixing bowl, blend 1 Tb. grated orange peel with ½ tsp. chili powder and 1 tsp. vegetable oil.

Put steaks on pan and broil for 5 minutes. Flip with tongs and broil 4 more minutes. Cut into one steak to check for desired doneness—continue broiling if necessary.

Turn off broiler, remove steaks and place on dinner plates. *Carefully* squeeze orange half over steaks and pick out seeds. Sprinkle with salt and pepper and serve.

Remove broiler pan and tray, line tray with aluminum foil and slide them back into oven 4"-6" from heat. Set oven to broil.

Carefully slash meat along fat at 1" intervals to prevent curling.

With a spoon, rub orange mixture over both sides of steaks.

Chew carefully. . . .

GOOD
Cut other half of orange into thin slices for garnish.

BETTER
Serve with New Potatoes Parmesan (page 86) and Ginger Carrots (page 87).

BEST
Plan ahead: buy a dozen oranges and squeeze fresh juice for her in the morning.

FROM THE VINEYARD
Cabernet Sauvignon, Medoc Bordeaux or Rioja

SHRIMP SCAMPI

This is no skimpy scampi.

Preparation Time
20-25 minutes

Cooking Time
9 minutes (plus rice)

Equipment Checklist
10″ non-stick frying pan, paring knife, medium saucepan with cover, medium mixing bowl, spatula, serving spoon

Power Shopping Guide
Seafood: ¾ lb. medium-sized fresh shrimp
Produce: 4 garlic cloves, 6 scallions, 1 fresh lemon
Seasoning: ground red pepper (cayenne), Worcestershire sauce, dried parsley flakes
Lube: olive oil
Misc: small box converted white rice, 1 stick butter, dry white wine

Serves 2

Buy fresh shrimp.

At low heat, melt 4 Tb. butter in frying pan. Stir in contents from mixing bowl. Increase heat to medium and stir occasionally until mixture bubbles (about 5 minutes).

Add shrimp to pan and stir occasionally until shrimp turn pink (3 minutes max). Remove from heat. Dinner is now ready—further cooking will result in rubber shrimp.

Before your guest arrives, prepare the shrimp (pages 135-136), cut up 6 scallions and mince 4 garlic cloves.

When she arrives, prepare 2 servings of rice using easy directions on box.

In mixing bowl, add minced garlic, sliced scallions, 1 tsp. olive oil, 2 tsp. lemon juice, 2 tsp. Worcestershire sauce, ¼ cup white wine, ⅛ tsp. red pepper and dash of parsley flakes. Begin next step 10 minutes before rice is ready.

Immediately tuck shrimp into bed of rice and spoon sauce over top.

Prepare yourself for the feast to come.

GOOD
Serve with fresh EATING IN Salad (page 90).

BETTER
Use seasoned rice instead of white rice.

BEST
Serve with warmed French bread to dip into savory garlic-butter sauce.

FROM THE VINEYARD
Fumé Blanc, Moselle Kabinett or German Rheingau Kabinett

HEN HOUSE ROCK

Your woman won't fly the coop if you serve these beautiful birds.

Preparation Time
15 minutes

Cooking Time
1¼ hours

Equipment Checklist
8″-square baking pan, medium saucepan with cover, paper towels

Power Shopping Guide
Meat: two 1½ lb. Rock Cornish game hens (if frozen, thaw ahead of time in refrigerator)
Misc: 1 box stuffing mix, small bag pre-chopped walnuts, raisins
Dairy: 1 stick butter
Seasoning: rosemary, salt, pepper

Serves 2

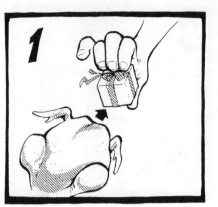

Remove free prize from inside of hens.

Rinse hens inside and out and pat dry with paper towels. Lightly salt and pepper inside.

Bake hens for 1 hour and 15 minutes.

Every 15 minutes, slip into kitchen and spoon hens with drippings from baking pan.

In saucepan, prepare 1 cup stuffing mix by following easy instructions on box. Then mix in 1½ Tb. chopped walnuts and a handful of raisins. Preheat oven to 350°.

Stuff hens, leaving some room for stuffing to expand. Lightly grease baking pan with butter and then add hens breast side-up.

In saucepan, melt 3 Tb. butter at low heat. Spoon butter on hens and sprinkle lightly with salt, pepper and rosemary.

After 5 spoonings, hens should be ready to eat.

GOOD
Serve with Mini Orange Carrots (page 86).

BETTER
Dice half a small apple and add to stuffing with walnuts and raisins.

BEST
Tell your date to arrive shortly before your hens are due out of the oven (unless you can keep up scintillating conversation for over an hour).

FROM THE VINEYARD
Pinot Noir or Moselle Kabinett

SAVORY SALMON with Creamy Cucumber Sauce

You don't have to swim upstream to spawn this sensational dish.

Preparation Time
10 minutes

Cooking Time
6-8 minutes

Equipment Checklist
Large pot, spatula, small mixing bowl, vegetable peeler, grater, paring knife, paper towels

Power Shopping Guide
Seafood: two 8-10 oz. fresh salmon fillets
Dairy: 1 cup plain (not vanilla) yogurt
Produce: 1 small fresh cucumber
Seasoning: sugar, ground white pepper, dried dill weed, salt
Misc: small bottle white wine vinegar

Serves 2

Call fish market in advance to see if they have fresh salmon fillets.

Fill large pot ⅔ full with water. Add ⅓ cup white wine vinegar and 1 tsp. salt. Bring to boil, then set heat to low so it simmers.

When water is barely simmering (under a boil), carefully slip salmon fillets into water with spatula.

7 EATING IN
Super Salmon Spotter

Perfect:
Salmon is juicy and slightly springy.
Underdone:
Squishy and fishy.
Overcooked:
Flaky and firm (see Chapter 13—Fancy Footwork for the botched meal).

Simmer salmon 6-8 minutes only.

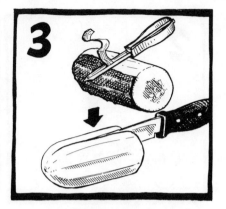

Meanwhile, cut cucumber in half crosswise. Peel one of the halves with a vegetable peeler and then cut it in half lengthwise.

With a teaspoon, scoop out and discard seeds from the peeled cucumber section and grate it. Use other cucumber section as a convenient cocktail garnish (page 127).

In mixing bowl, add grated cucumber, ¼ tsp. white pepper, ¼ tsp. salt, ¼ tsp. sugar and ¼ tsp. dill weed. Glop in 1 cup plain yogurt and mix thoroughly. Sauce is ready.

If salmon is ready for dinner before you, simply remove pot from heat—you can leave the fillets in water for up to 15 minutes without fear of overcooking.

To serve, remove salmon from pot with spatula and place on paper towels to dry. Transfer to dinner plates and spoon sauce evenly over top of salmon. Sprinkle lightly with dill weed.

GOOD
Serve with Rice 'n' 'Shrooms (page 91) and a salad.

BETTER
Save time: prepare sauce in advance and chill. Or simmer salmon in advance, refrigerate and serve chilled.

BEST
Refrigerate leftover salmon and serve it on her bagels in the morning!

FROM THE VINEYARD
Sauvignon Blanc or Riesling Kabinett

73

CHICKEN MARSALA

You'll melt, along with the Parmesan cheese, over these tender breasts.

Preparation Time
10 minutes

Cooking Time
12 minutes

Equipment Checklist
10″ non-stick frying pan with cover, spatula, paring knife, paper towels

Power Shopping Guide
Meat: 4 fresh boneless chicken breast halves
Dairy: 1 stick butter, small canister grated Parmesan cheese
Produce: 1 garlic clove, ¼ lb. fresh mushrooms, 1 fresh lemon
Seasoning: dried basil, salt, pepper
Pasta: 16 oz. package linguine noodles
Misc: small bottle dry Marsala wine, small bag all-purpose flour

Serves 2

Ask your friendly grocer for the freshest breasts on hand.

Split and rinse chicken breasts and remove any skin. Dry breasts on paper towels. Slice mushrooms and mince 1 garlic clove (page 135). Begin cooking linguine according to directions on box.

Flip breasts with spatula and re-season with salt, pepper and basil. Add 1 clove minced garlic and sliced mushrooms.

Slowly pour ½ cup Marsala wine around breasts, add 1 tsp. lemon juice and cook 3-4 more minutes. See if the noodles are ready.

Put ½ cup flour on a clean plate and massage breasts in flour until all sides are coated. Then set aside.

At low heat, melt 4 Tb. butter in frying pan. Don't burn the butter!

Add flour-coated breasts to pan and lightly sprinkle with salt, pepper and basil. Increase heat to medium and fry chicken until golden brown (4-5 minutes).

Spoon 1 Tb. grated Parmesan over each breast. Cover pan till cheese melts. Dinner's ready when you cut into center of one breast and it's white throughout. Patch gash with melted cheese.

Make a bed of linguine on each plate, tuck in breasts and top with mushrooms and savory sauce. Jump in!

GOOD
Serve with a fresh EATING IN Salad (page 90).

BETTER
Serve with warmed French bread and butter.

BEST
Grate your own fresh *parmigiano reggiano* cheese.

FROM THE VINEYARD
Côtes du Rhône

SONNY'S SECRET SPAGHETTI SAUCE

We had to sneak this Family recipe past the Godfather so you can be an Italian Scallion.

Preparation Time
8 minutes

Cooking Time
40 minutes (minimum)

Equipment Checklist
Two 4-6 quart pots with covers, colander, stirring spoon, can opener

Power Shopping Guide
Canned goods: 28 oz. can crushed tomatoes, 12 oz. can tomato paste, 15 oz. can tomato sauce
Meat: 1 lb. fresh ground beef
Produce: 2 green peppers, 1 large onion, 4 garlic cloves, ½ lb. fresh mushrooms
Seasoning: oregano, salt, pepper
Misc: 16 oz. package spaghetti noodles, small canister grated Parmesan cheese

Serves 2 (with lots of leftover sauce)

In large pot, break 1 lb. ground beef into chunks. Set burner to medium-low, stir meat and cook until it's no longer pink.

While meat is browning, slice 2 green peppers into bite-sized chunks (discard stems and seeds). Peel and dice onion. Slice mushrooms. Mince 4 garlic cloves. (page 135).

When dinner date arrives, prepare spaghetti noodles in second pot, according to directions on box. Then drain noodles into colander placed in sink.

Add portions of hot spaghetti to dinner plates, cover with Sonny's Secret Sauce and serve with grated Parmesan cheese in bowl.

5 EATING IN Spaghetti Spot

Two delicious portions.

Drain off fat from meat. Return pot to burner. Toss all ingredients into pot (except noodles and cheese) and stir at medium heat. (Hint: open cans first for more tomato taste.)

When sauce begins to bubble, cover pot, reduce heat to low and simmer for at least 30 minutes, stirring occasionally. Add salt, pepper and oregano to taste.

Calculate 2 spaghetti portions by standing a fistful of spaghetti noodles on circle. (*Hint:* system works better *before* boiling noodles. . . .)

You'll have enough sauce to serve yourself, your date, the Consiglieri, Sonny, The Godfather, Michael, a bodyguard, Luca and the Chief.

GOOD
Serve with Italian Garlic Bread (page 89) and an EATING IN Salad (page 90).

BETTER
Try shells or elbow macaroni instead of spaghetti to avoid unsavory slurping noises.

BEST
For a spicy variation, substitute 1 lb. hot Italian sausage sliced in 1″ pieces for ground beef in Step 1.

FROM THE VINEYARD
Chianti or Zinfandel

STEAK (Her Name Here)

Formerly called "Steak Diane," she'll appreciate this feast you've named especially for her. (And you'll never have to explain who Diane is.)

Preparation Time
4 minutes

Cooking Time
14 minutes

Equipment Checklist
10" non-stick frying pan, Chef's knife, tongs, small saucepan, matches

Power Shopping Guide
Meat: two ¾"-thick boneless ½-¾ lb. Delmonico (or Porterhouse or Sirloin) steaks
Produce: 6 scallions
Condiment: small bottle Worcestershire sauce
Seasoning: ground (powdered) mustard, pepper, dried parsley flakes
Liquor: bottle or miniature of cognac
Dairy: 1 stick butter

Serves 2

Trim any excess fat from around edges of steaks. Then cut up 6 scallions (page 135).

At low heat, melt 2 Tb. butter to coat frying pan. Then add steaks and raise heat to medium-high. Sear (brown) 1-2 minutes on each side and set burner back to low.

For flambé: Warm 1½ oz. cognac in small saucepan at low heat. Dim house lights.

At the table, carefully ignite cognac with match and slowly pour blue flames over steaks. *Voila!*

Remove steaks from pan and set aside on clean plate.

When pan cools down, stir in: 1 Tb. ground mustard, pre-cut scallions, 2 Tb. Worcestershire sauce and a dash of pepper. Simmer and stir for 2 minutes.

Return steaks to pan, increase to medium heat, and cook on each side to desired doneness (about 4 minutes each side for medium-rare). Then transfer steaks to dinner plates and top with sauce from pan.

For runaway flambé: Don't panic! Just leave pan alone and flames will quickly die down. If there is any danger of a fire, cover pan with lid.

After the fireworks, sprinkle steaks with parsley flakes and a dash of pepper. Serve immediately!

GOOD
For a unique taste, add 2 Tb. oyster sauce at Step 4.

BETTER
Serve with Twice Baked Stuffed Spuds (page 88) and Mini Orange Carrots (page 86).

BEST
Put dog outside.

FROM THE VINEYARD
Cabernet Sauvignon or Zinfandel

OPENING NIGHT FLOUNDER

The perfect dinner to catch before the performance.

Preparation Time
5 minutes

Cooking Time
6 minutes

Equipment Checklist
10″ non-stick frying pan,
spatula, paper towels

Power Shopping Guide
Seafood: ¾ - 1 lb. fresh
flounder fillets (if frozen, thaw
ahead of time in refrigerator)
Produce: ¼ lb. fresh
mushrooms, 6 scallions,
1 garlic clove, 1 lemon
Lube: olive oil, stick of
margarine
Seasoning: dried tarragon,
dried parsley flakes, pepper
Misc: small bag all-purpose
flour

Serves 2

Cast around for 2 fresh
flounder fillets.

Cut up 6 scallions and
mushrooms and mince 1 garlic
clove (pages 135-136). Cut
lemon into 4 wedges.

EATING IN
Official Doneness Tester

Perfect:
Fish is slightly opaque when
you slit into thickest portion.

Underdone:
Fish flaps around on plate.

Overcooked:
Flaky and breaky (see Chapter
13—Fancy Footwork for the
botched meal).

Lower burner to medium heat
and melt 2 Tb. margarine in
same pan. Add sliced
mushrooms, scallions, minced
garlic, dash each of tarragon
and pepper. Sauté (stir) for 2
minutes.

3

Measure ¼ cup all-purpose flour onto wide plate and mix with ½ tsp. pepper. Pat fish dry with paper towels. Then place fillets in flour and flip to fully coat both sides.

4

Coat frying pan with 2 Tb. olive oil and set burner to medium-high. When oil is rippling hot, carefully add fillets in single layer.

5

Fry on one side about 2 minutes until fillets are golden-brown. With spatula and a fork, gently flip fillets and fry two more minutes. When fillets are perfect, transfer to dinner plates.

7

Remove pan from heat. Squeeze juice from one lemon wedge into mixture and stir, then pour equally over fillets. Garnish each fillet with a lemon wedge and sprinkle lightly with parsley flakes.

8

It may be curtains for them, but it's show time for you.

GOOD
Accompany with Rice 'n' 'Shrooms (page 91)

BETTER
Serve with Mini Orange Carrots (page 86).

BEST
Dust off your casting couch for the next catch of the day.

FROM THE VINEYARD
Chardonnay or Sauvignon Blanc

Hot HAWAIIAN LUAU

Experience the thrill of Hawaii at home while you slice, dice and entice.

Preparation Time
15 minutes

Cooking Time
4 minutes (plus rice)

Equipment Checklist
10″ non-stick frying pan with cover, Chef's knife, spatula, small and large mixing bowls, medium saucepan with cover, can opener, chopsticks (optional)

Power Shopping Guide
Canned goods: 8 oz. can chunk pineapple in natural juice
Produce: 2 garlic cloves, 1 red bell pepper, 1 green pepper, 2 small carrots, 6 scallions
Seasoning: ground ginger
Lube: vegetable oil
Misc: small bottle soy sauce, small box corn starch, small box converted white rice

Serves 2

Spread sand across your entire living room, turn on your Don Ho videos and strum along on your authentic ukulele.

In medium saucepan, start two servings of rice according to directions on package.

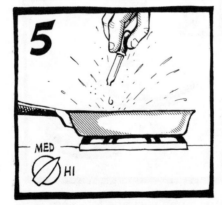

When rice is ready (keep it covered), pour 1½ Tb. oil into frying pan and set burner to medium-high. Let oil get rippling hot—a drop of water will spatter when oil is ready. Tilt pan to coat with oil.

Carefully add contents of large mixing bowl. Stir for 2 minutes. Then reduce heat to low and pour in sauce from small mixing bowl. Toss for 1 minute and remove from heat.

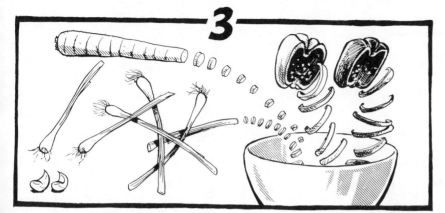

Rinse vegetables. Slice green and red peppers in half (discard stems and seeds, and save half of each pepper for a sunrise luau). Cut remaining halves into thin strips. Peel and slice 2 carrots into thin disks. Cut up scallions (page 135). Mince two garlic cloves. Put everything into large mixing bowl.

Into small mixing bowl, strain ⅓ cup pineapple juice from can (drain rest of juice into mouth). Then stir in 1 tsp. ginger, 1 Tb. corn starch and 3 Tb. soy sauce. Add pineapple chunks to the *large* bowl.

Place one portion of rice on each dinner plate, top with Hot Hawaiian stir-fry and serve with chopsticks (make sure you've practiced first).

If you've done everything right, she'll wanna hula after dinner.

GOOD
Start off with Amazing Shortcut Soup (page 52), such as cream of broccoli.

BETTER
For a meatier taste, dice ⅓ lb. tofu (drained) into 1″ squares and pat dry. After Step 5, sauté tofu in hot oil for 6 minutes (or until lightly browned) and then continue recipe.

BEST
Wear your best Hawaiian shirt and have a lei waiting for her.

FROM THE VINEYARD
Gewürztraminer

CHAPTER 9
A LITTLE ON THE SIDE

Whip up a little dish on the side that will satisfy even insatiable cravings.

A side dish or two not only provides your minimum daily adult requirements, but adds flavor, variety and color to the main dish.

Each EATING IN main dish comes with helpful suggestions for tasty side dishes to complement your meal—and they're designed to prevent stressful cooking area overload.

You can also pick up your favorite easy-to-prepare side dishes at the grocery store. Or easier yet, buy a fresh-made side dish at a deli and toss out the container.

Remember, when it comes to dinner, a little on the side never hurt anyone.

Don't panic if she asks about the side dish you picked up at a deli. Just tell her it's your grandma's secret recipe.

New Potatoes Parmesan

Studs McKenzie's favorite spuds.

Preparation Time
2 minutes

Cooking Time
15 minutes

Equipment Checklist
Medium saucepan with cover

Power Shopping Guide
Produce: 6 golf ball-sized red or new potatoes
Dairy: butter, grated Parmesan cheese
Seasoning: salt, dried parsley flakes

1. Rinse potatoes and place in medium saucepan. Add enough cold water to cover them completely. Add 1 tsp. salt. (If potatoes are baseball-sized, cut 3 into uniform wedges.)
2. Set burner to medium heat and bring to boil. Cook until potatoes pierce easily with a fork (about 10 minutes after water boils).
3. Use cover to drain water into sink. Dot potatoes with slivers of butter and sprinkle with 2 Tb. grated Parmesan cheese. Cover. Potatoes will stay hot until rest of your meal is ready. Transfer to serving plate and sprinkle with parsley flakes.

Mini Orange Carrots

Baby carrots with a big orange taste.

Preparation Time
2 minutes

Cooking Time
10 minutes or less

Equipment Checklist
Medium saucepan with cover, paring knife

Power Shopping Guide
Produce: small bag of baby carrots
Dairy: small container of orange juice, butter
Seasoning: small box of brown sugar

1. Scrub 12 baby carrots under cold water. Cut off tops.
2. Place carrots in medium saucepan and cover with water. Boil 10 minutes or until carrots pierce easily with a fork. Use cover to drain water into sink. Place carrots in serving bowl.
3. In same saucepan, melt 2 Tb. butter at low heat. Add ¼ cup of o.j. and 2 Tb. brown sugar. Mix until slightly thickened—about 1-2 minutes. Pour over carrots and serve hot.

Ginger Carrots

A very popular dish on Gilligan's Island.

Preparation Time
5 minutes

Cooking Time
12-17 minutes

Equipment Checklist
Vegetable steamer, vegetable peeler, covered saucepan, paring knife

Power Shopping Guide
Produce: 2 medium-sized carrots
Dairy: butter
Seasoning: ground ginger, salt, pepper

1. Peel carrots with vegetable peeler. Cut carrots into ⅛-inch disks.

2. Put ¾ inch of water and steamer into saucepan. Load carrot disks onto steamer and cover. Set burner to medium heat and bring to boil.

3. Steam carrots until tender—about 12-17 minutes—and turn off heat. Remove steamer from pan, pour off liquid and return carrots to pan. Top with 1 Tb. butter, 1 tsp. ground ginger and salt and pepper to taste. Mix and cover until ready to serve with main course.

Broc Around The Clock

So tasty it even inspired a song.

Preparation Time
3 minutes

Cooking Time
10-12 minutes (until tender-crisp)

Equipment Checklist
Vegetable steamer, medium saucepan with cover, paring knife

Power Shopping Guide
Produce: 1 stalk broccoli, 1 lemon
Dairy: butter
Seasoning: salt and pepper

1. Buy fresh, firm, dark green broccoli. Remove large leaves and chop off woody stems. Cut broccoli florets into bite-sized pieces and rinse in cold water.

2. Put ¾ inch water and steamer into saucepan. Load broccoli onto steamer and cover. Set burner to medium heat and bring to boil.

3. Steam broccoli until tender—about 10-12 minutes. Put on serving plate, dot with slivers of butter, and sprinkle with lemon juice, salt and pepper.

Stir-Fried Garlic Green Beans

Exposes the green giant in you.

Preparation Time
3 minutes

Cooking Time
4-5 minutes

Equipment Checklist
Frying pan, non-metal mixing spoon

Power Shopping Guide
Produce: ½ lb. fresh green beans, 2 garlic cloves
Lube: small jar of vegetable oil
Seasoning: small package of slivered almonds, pepper

1. Rinse beans in cold water. Snap off ends and discard. Snap beans in half.

2. Mince 2 garlic cloves (page 135). Add 1 Tb. vegetable oil in frying pan and set to high heat. When oil ripples, add green beans and minced garlic. Stir continuously for 3-4 minutes.

3. Transfer beans to serving dish. Sprinkle with slivered almonds and pepper. Serve hot.

Twice-Baked Spuds

Knock the stuffing out of them. And pack it back in.

Preparation Time
5 minutes

Cooking Time
1 hour plus 20 minutes

Equipment Checklist
Fork, knife, spoon, mixing bowl, grater

Power Shopping Guide
Produce: 2 medium-sized baking potatoes
Dairy: butter, small container of fresh milk, small hunk of cheddar cheese
Seasoning: pepper, salt

1. Preheat oven to 400°. Rinse potatoes and prick in several places with fork. Place on rack in middle of oven. Bake for 1 hour.

2. With oven mitts, remove potatoes from oven. Cut a thin, lengthwise strip into each potato. Keep on the mitts and spoon out ¾ of potato pulp without breaking skin. Put scoopings into mixing bowl.

3. Grate ½ cup of cheddar cheese. Add grated cheese, 3 Tb. milk and 2 Tb. butter into mixing bowl and season with salt and pepper to taste. Mash with fork till blended. Restuff potatoes and rebake for 20 minutes (or until filling is golden).

Hot Buttered Beer Bread

The bread that made Milwaukee famous.

Preparation Time
5 minutes

Cooking Time
40 minutes

Equipment Checklist
Cheap aluminum bread loaf pan (approx. 8½" x 4½" x 2½"), mixing bowl, mixing spoon, paper towels

Power Shopping Guide
Beer: 12 oz. can of your favorite beer
Seasoning: small bag of *self-rising* flour, sugar, vegetable oil

1. Heat oven to 350°. With a paper towel, coat entire inside of bread pan with 1 Tb. vegetable oil.
2. In mixing bowl, use mixing spoon to thoroughly combine 3 cups *self-rising* flour with 3 Tb. sugar and 1 can of beer. Moosh dough into bread pan. Shove in oven.
3. Bake for 40 minutes or until golden brown on top. Pop loaf out of pan and cool for a few minutes before serving to make slicing easier. Serve with butter.

Zesty Garlic Bread

Custom made for Italian or French bread. Make sure both of you eat it.

Preparation Time
5 minutes

Cooking Time
8-10 minutes

Equipment Checklist
Serrated knife, baking pan, aluminum foil

Power Shopping Guide
Bread: loaf of fresh Italian or French bread (no Wonder or Matzo, please)
Produce: small jar minced garlic
Dairy: 1 stick butter

1. Cut half the loaf into 1" slices, but not quite through to the bottom.
2. Smear small amount of minced garlic into each bread gash. Then place a thin sliver of butter into each gash. Set oven for 350°.
3. Wrap bread in aluminum foil, place on baking pan and shove into oven for 8-10 minutes. Make sure it doesn't burn.

HEALTHY SALADS

Salads are not only good for you—they also provide the roughage that keeps you moving.

Preparing a fresh, tangy salad takes only a minute, if you know this secret:

Simply drop by the nearest grocery store or fast food salad bar and save yourself all the rinsing, cutting and waste. Then transfer into salad bowls, toss out the plastic containers and tell her you picked everything yourself.

If there are no salad bars handy, plan on spending a few more minutes. Be sure to buy only fresh produce. Avoid yellow, wilted or dry outer lettuce leaves. Rinse everything thoroughly under cold water (especially spinach and squash) and shake dry. Cut vegetables—and tear inner lettuce leaves—into bite-sized pieces.

EATING IN Salad

Iceberg or romaine lettuce leaves with any of the following: sliced tomato, fresh mushroom slices, onion slices, croutons, cucumbers, cheese chunks, raisins, alfalfa sprouts, nuts and whatever else you like.

Spinach Salad

Spinach leaves, red onion slices, bacon bits, fresh mushroom slices, croutons.

Who-Made-the-Salad? Salad

Equal amounts of spinach and Boston lettuce leaves, thinly sliced radishes, cherry tomatoes (halved) and sectioned orange slices.

SALAD DRESSINGS

Available in any grocery store. Toss salad with dressing in kitchen and hide the bottle. At the table, sprinkle with freshly ground pepper from a pepper mill.

QUICKIES ON THE SIDE

Cheese 'n' Butter Linguine

Prepare linguine according to directions on package (see page 77 for portion size). Drain. While hot, mix with 1 Tb. butter and toss with 2 Tb. grated Parmesan cheese. Add salt and pepper to taste.

Miami Rice

Prepare white rice according to directions on package. Then heat 1 cup canned black beans in medium saucepan. Drain and transfer to serving bowl. Spoon beans on top of rice on plate.

Rice 'n' Shrooms

Slice ¼ lb. mushrooms (page 136). Then melt 2 Tb. butter in medium saucepan at medium heat. Sauté (stir) sliced mushrooms for 2 minutes, add ⅔ cup uncooked long-grain white rice and stir until rice is golden (about 5 minutes.) Add 1⅓ cups water and a dash of salt and pepper. Increase heat until mixture boils, then cover, reduce heat to low and simmer for 20 minutes. Rice is ready when all water is absorbed. Add a pinch of dried parsley flakes, toss with fork and serve.

DESIGNER FLAVORED BUTTERS

Served in their own shot glass

Honey Butter

Bring ½ stick of butter to room temperature. Mash with fork in shallow mixing bowl. Add 1 Tb. honey and mash again. Scoop into 2 shot glasses and serve.

Garlic Butter

Bring ½ stick of butter to room temperature. Mash with fork in shallow mixing bowl. Add 1 clove minced garlic and sprinkle with 1 tsp. parsley. Mash again. Scoop into 2 shot glasses and serve.

CHAPTER 10

AFTERPLAY

Cap off your perfect dinner with a sinful dessert she'll remember for years to come.

Y ou've already spent more time in the kitchen today than you have in the past year. So why return to that hot kitchen to slave over an extravagant dessert?

You can whip up most of these refreshing desserts ahead of time, or in a matter of minutes. Then you can get back to the business at hand. And shut down your kitchen till morning.

Chef Tell's Favorite

One 10 oz. package frozen raspberries in syrup • ⅛ cup sugar • premium vanilla ice cream • 1 Tb. corn starch • Framboise (raspberry liqueur) • sweetened whipped cream.

Thaw raspberries. Drain syrup into a small saucepan, stir in ⅛ cup sugar and boil at low heat. In a small mixing bowl, dissolve 1 Tb. corn starch in 1 Tb. water. Pour into boiling syrup and stir until mixture thickens. Add raspberries and 2 Tb. Framboise and heat until bubbly. Remove from heat.

Scoop vanilla ice cream into dessert dishes. Pour hot raspberry mixture over the ice cream. Top with whipped cream and serve immediately! (Or prepare sauce mixture in advance, refrigerate in covered saucepan, and reheat when ready to indulge.)

Peaches Pistachio

4 peach halves (canned) and 1 pint pistachio ice cream ● raspberry brandy.

Drain syrup off 4 peach halves. Place 2 halves in each serving dish and top with scoop pistachio ice cream. Pour a shot of raspberry brandy on top and serve.

Amaretto Been Berry Berry Good To Me

1 pint fresh strawberries ● ½ pint fresh blueberries ● almond slivers ● Amaretto liqueur.

Rinse strawberries and remove stem with your fingernail. Rinse blueberries. Add berries into bowl (discard the mushy ones) pour in 1 cup Amaretto. Cover and refrigerate 2-3 hours. To serve, spoon into dessert cup, and sprinkle with almond slivers. A winner!

Chocolate-Dipped Strawberries

1 pint fresh strawberries ● ½ cup semi-sweet chocolate morsels ● waxed paper ● medium-sized saucepan with cover.

Add 2″ of water to saucepan and boil. Meanwhile, rinse and pat strawberries dry. When water boils, reduce to simmer. Set cover upside-down on saucepan (instant double boiler!) and add ½ cup chocolate morsels into center. Stir until chocolate is smooth. Hold strawberries by stem and dip ⅔ into hot chocolate. Place on plate covered with waxed paper. Refrigerate till hard. Serve when ready. For a real treat, feed each other à la *9½ Weeks.*

Chocolate Pear Cups

1 pint vanilla ice cream ● 2 pear halves (canned) ● chocolate syrup.

Place 1 pear half in each dessert cup. Fill center with 1 scoop vanilla ice cream. Top with chocolate syrup.

Hot Vermont Weekend

1 pint vanilla ice cream ● *real maple syrup* ● *chopped walnuts*
● *Maraschino cherries.*

Heat ⅓ cup maple syrup in small saucepan. Scoop vanilla ice cream into 2 dessert cups and pour on the hot maple syrup. Sprinkle with chopped walnuts and top with a cherry. It's Larry, Darryl and Darryl's favorite!

Kahlua Volcano

2 shots Kahlua ● *1 pint of your favorite ice cream* ● *chopped walnuts*
● *2 Maraschino cherries.*

Scoop ice cream into dessert dish. Shape ice cream into volcano. Pour 1 shot Kahula into crater in center of volcano. Sprinkle with chopped walnuts and top with maraschino cherry.

Kahlua Krakatoa

Same as above, but substitute cherry bomb for maraschino cherry. Light fuse. Run away.

Just Desserts

Stop off at your favorite bakery on the way home from work. Buy two of the most luscious desserts you can find. Tell her you baked them just for her.

SURGEON GENERAL'S WARNING: Practicing Safe Sex Substantially Increases The Likelihood Of A Healthy And Happy Life For Both Of You.

CHAPTER 11

AFTERGLOW

Feed each other these delicious pick-me-back-ups for mouth-watering treats after midnight.

You must be doing something right if both of you are basking in the afterglow. Now's your chance to spring your next to last surprise on her. Try one of these late-night delights guaranteed to keep both of you going till the crack of dawn.

Fresh Fruit Bowl

Rinse and chill your favorite in-season fruits in a decorative bowl. Or serve more exotic fruits like kiwi, papaya and mangoes.

Strawberries in Champagne

Rinse a half dozen small-to-medium sized strawberries. Place in chilled champagne glasses. Fill with champagne. Cheers!

Chocolate Truffles

Plan ahead. Stop off at your local gourmet or chocolate shoppe and buy them on your way home. You'll be glad you did.

Cordials

Pour your favorite liqueur into a cordial glass (or your favorite navel). Try serving Amaretto, Grand Marnier, Cointreau or Framboise.

CHAPTER 12

THE MORNING AFTER

Wake up your woman with a hot breakfast that will fulfill her wildest dreams.

Pop open a bottle of chilled champagne first thing in the morning and you'll begin the day with a bang. Especially when you arouse her taste buds with the aroma of your bountiful breakfast wafting into the room.

And who says romance is dead?

However, if you're not prepared, your Breakfast Special will be nothing more than a hearty swig of Listerine and a hurried goodbye.

If you've helped her build up a healthy appetite, you can satisfy her once again with a tempting breakfast. But don't get caught with your pants down—stock all the breakfast ingredients you need *in advance*.

Unless you think she'd prefer cold pizza and warm beer, stock up on fresh eggs, bread, o.j. and champagne. Or surprise her with a *real* treat and prepare one of the incredible breakfast recipes in this chapter. And have a nice day.

Until Domino's delivers hot breakfasts and mimosas, make sure you stock up on fresh ingredients and champagne just in case. . .

Open Your Eyes To These Refreshing EATING IN Eye-Openers

Screwdriver
1 shot vodka and fresh o.j. on ice. Stir. Serve in wine glass and garnish with an orange slice.

Raspberry Royale
Add ½ tsp. raspberry liqueur to glass of chilled champagne. Stir gently. Mmmmmm.

Grand Mimosa
Add ½ oz. Grand Marnier to chilled champagne containing enough o.j. to make it opaque. Serve in wine glass over ice.

Breakfast in Bed
Shake 1 shot brandy, 1 shot vodka, 3 oz. grapefruit juice and ice cubes in cocktail shaker. Strain into wine glass. It's all the nourishment you need.

Fuzzy Navel
Add ½ oz. peach schnapps to fresh o.j. over ice. Serve in champagne glass and garnish with orange wedge.

California Sunshine
50/50 mix of pink champagne and o.j. plus 1 dash crème de cassis on ice. Stir.

Or try one of these tasty non-alcohol drinks:

Flying Fruit
Cut up ½ cup of orange and melon slices. Add to two wine glasses and pour in chilled pineapple juice.

Cranberry Club
Add ice cubes into tall glass. Fill glass ⅔-full with cranberry juice. Add 1 tsp. sweetened lime juice and top with club soda. Stir.

Keep Your Eyes Open With These Piping Hot Coffee Concoctions

You don't need Joe DiMaggio to help you make your coffee. Whichever brewing system you use, start with 1 heaping tablespoon ground coffee for each ¾ cup water and adjust to taste. Then try one of the following recipes and let 'er rip.

For an extra added attraction, top your coffee drinks with shavings of white or dark chocolate. Simply use a dull knife or grater—not your Trak II.

Irish Coffee
Rinse out 2 wine glasses with very hot water. Add 2 tsp. sugar, 1 shot Irish Whiskey and strong hot coffee to each. Stir. Top with whipped cream and enjoy.

Kahlua 'n' Caffeine
Add 1 shot of Kahlua into coffee mug. Fill with hot black coffee and top with whipped cream.

Mucho Macho Mocha
In a medium saucepan, heat and stir: 2 cups milk, 6 tsp. cocoa powder, 3 tsp. instant coffee powder, 2 tsp. sugar, 4 Tb. Kahlua. Just *before* it begins to boil, pour into 2 coffee mugs. Top with whipped cream and sprinkle with cinnamon.

Keoki Coffee
Pour one shot brandy and one shot Kahlua into coffee cup. Fill cup with hot black coffee and stir.

Latin Leprechaun
Add ½ shot of Kahlua and ½ shot Bailey's Irish Creme into coffee cup. Fill cup with hot black coffee and stir.

Hollywood Hot
Add ½ shot Grand Marnier to a cup of hot tea. Garnish with a cinnamon stick.

SCRAMBLED EGGS IMPERIAL

Eat like royalty first thing in the morning.

Preparation Time
5 minutes

Cooking Time
8 minutes

Equipment Checklist
10″ non-stick frying pan, medium mixing bowl, paring knife, plastic spatula

Power Shopping Guide
Dairy: 4 large fresh eggs, milk, butter, 2 oz. chunk of cheddar cheese (½ cup)
Produce: 6 fresh mushrooms, 1 small onion, 1 green pepper
Seasoning: salt and pepper

Serves 2

Break eggs into mixing bowl. Add ¼ cup milk and beat with fork until well-blended (pick out shell fragments).

Dice onion and slice mushrooms (page 136). Rinse green pepper, cut in half (discard stem and seeds) and dice one of the halves.

VARIATIONS

Substitute the following ingredients and enjoy delicious variations first thing in the morning.

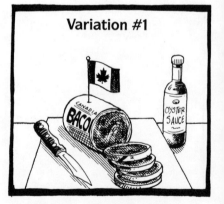

Variation #1

Sauté four Canadian Bacon slices cut into bite-sized pieces at Step 3. At Step 4, add 1 Tb. oyster sauce to eggs.

Over medium heat, melt 1 Tb. butter in frying pan. Add onions and green pepper pieces and sauté (stir) for 4 minutes. Add mushrooms and sauté 2 more minutes.

Reduce heat to medium-low. Pour egg mixture into pan. Grate cheddar cheese on top and add a dash of salt and pepper. With spatula, push eggs from the outside edge toward center to cook evenly, and turn them over to scramble.

When eggs look ready to eat (4-5 minutes), remove from heat and serve.

Variation #2

Variation #3

At Step 4, instead of cheddar, add half a 3 ounce package of cream cheese with chives (cut into pieces) into pan with eggs.

Now that you've got the hang of it, add whatever you damn well please to customize your Scrambled Eggs Imperial.

GOOD
Serve with buttered English Muffins.

BETTER
Serve with freshly squeezed orange juice

BEST
Add champagne to your freshly squeezed o.j. to make Mimosas.

THE MORNING AFTER PANCAKE

Prepare one giant pancake instead of six and spend your time with her instead of the stove.

Preparation Time
6 minutes

Cooking Time
20 minutes

Equipment Checklist
Round non-stick frying pan, screwdriver, medium mixing bowl, whisk, 2 spatulas, oven mitt

Power Shopping Guide
Dairy: 2 fresh eggs, milk, butter
Produce: 1 ripe banana
Seasoning: small bag of chopped walnuts, cinnamon, salt, small bottle vanilla extract, small bag of all-purpose flour, pancake syrup

Serves 2

Use screwdriver to remove plastic handle from frying pan to prevent a melt-down in your oven (or use an 8½" round cake pan instead).

In mixing bowl, break 2 eggs and add 1 cup flour, 1 cup milk, 1 tsp. cinnamon, 1 tsp. vanilla, 2 Tb. chopped walnuts and dash salt. Whisk till smooth. Preheat oven to 375° and peel and slice your banana.

Wake your date gingerly.

After 20 minutes, when pancake is puffy on the edges and golden brown in the center, remove pan from oven, then lift pancake from pan with 2 spatulas and place on serving plate.

In pan, melt 2 Tb. butter at low heat—don't burn butter. Tilt pan to coat sides. (*Hint:* use oven mitt.)

Turn off burner and slowly pour batter into center of pan—don't stir. Top evenly with banana slices. Place pan in center of oven for 20 minutes.

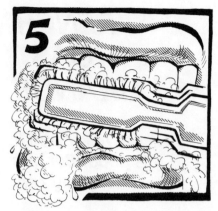

Brush your teeth vigorously.

Cut into quarters and serve with maple syrup and butter.

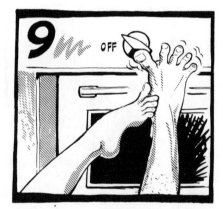

Turn off oven. Make your own heat.

GOOD
Serve with *real* maple syrup—warmed.

BETTER
Drain ¾ cup frozen, canned or fresh blueberries and substitute for banana and walnuts.

BEST
Serve with a frosty Raspberry Royale (page 100).

FRENCH TOAST À L'ORANGE

The French never had it this good. But you certainly can.

Preparation Time
5 minutes

Cooking Time
5 minutes

Equipment Checklist
10″ non-stick frying pan, large mixing bowl, grater, spatula, whisk, measuring spoons

Power Shopping Guide
Dairy: 4 large fresh eggs, 1 stick butter
Bakery: 1 loaf French, Italian or cinnamon-raisin bread (sliced ¾″-1¼″-thick)
Produce: 1 fresh navel orange
Seasoning: small bottle vanilla extract, ground cinnamon, ground nutmeg, pancake syrup

Serves 2

1 Know when it's time to get away from the heat and into the kitchen.

2 Rinse and dry orange. Lightly grate 1 Tb. orange peel and cut orange in half.

6 Dunk one slice of bread in bowl. Soak on one side for a couple of seconds, flip and soak again.

7 Transfer slice to hot pan. Begin another slice at Step 6. Fry each slice until golden brown, flip, and brown other side.

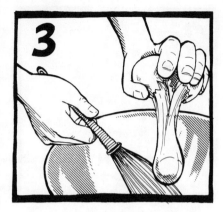

In large mixing bowl, break 4 eggs and beat thoroughly with whisk.

Squeeze juice from one orange half into mixing bowl (watch for falling seeds) and add 1 tsp. cinnamon, ¼ tsp. nutmeg, 1 tsp. vanilla and 1 Tb. orange gratings. Beat mixture again.

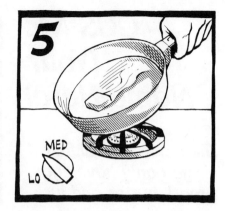

Melt 1 Tb. butter in frying pan over medium-low heat. Tilt pan to coat inside completely.

Place french toast on plate and serve hot! Re-whisk batter and repeat Steps 5, 6 & 7 until batter is finished or you're full. Be sure to keep the syrup on your plate and off your date.

GOOD
Cut other half of orange into wedges to serve as garnish.

BETTER
Serve with *real* maple syrup—warmed.

BEST
Complete the meal with crisp Bakin' Bacon (page 111).

*E*GGS Mc (*Your Name Here*)

The perfect breakfast if you only have eggs, bread, butter and luck.

Preparation Time
2 minutes

Cooking Time
4 minutes

Equipment Checklist
10″ non-stick frying pan, plastic spatula

Power Shopping Guide
Dairy: 4 fresh eggs, butter
Bakery: loaf of white or wheat bread

Serves 2

What do you do when both you and the refrigerator are practically bare?

Place 2 bread slices butter-side-up in frying pan in single layer. Gently break one egg into center of each bread slice.

After 3 minutes, check doneness by lifting edge of bread with spatula. When bread turns golden brown, flip *gently* without breaking yolk.

Cut, tear or bite out a silver-dollar size hole in the center of 4 bread slices.

Butter one side of each slice.

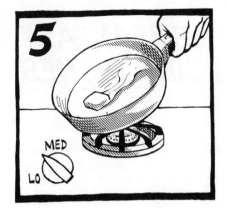

Melt 1 Tb. butter in frying pan at medium-low heat and coat inside of pan.

After 1 minute, check under edge of bread. Remove from pan at desired doneness and flip over onto serving plate. Repeat Steps 5-8 for two more servings.

GOOD
Garnish with orange wedges.

BETTER
Serve with Bakin' Bacon (page 111).

BEST
Serve with chilled California Sunshine (page 100) and loads of coffee.

BREAKFAST SIDE DISHES

Homemade Hash Browns

Put these potatoes in your pipe and smoke 'em.

Preparation Time
5 minutes

Cooking Time
20 aromatic minutes

Equipment Checklist
10″ non-stick frying pan, spatula, paring knife, mixing bowl

Power Shopping Guide
Produce: 2 medium-sized potatoes (cut out the eyes, ears, wrinkles and green skin), 1 small onion
Dairy: butter
Seasoning: all-purpose flour, salt and pepper

1. Dice potatoes to size of dice and put in mixing bowl. Sprinkle with 1½ Tb. flour and mix.
2. Chop onion. Melt 3 Tb. butter in frying pan at low heat. Add onion, increase heat to medium and sauté until light brown. Add potatoes to pan and stir. Add salt and pepper and stir until brown and tender (about 15-20 minutes).
3. When potatoes are nearly ready, heap in pile in center, turn heat to medium-high, and brown bottom till crispy. Flip pile and repeat. Serve hot!

Fresh Fruit Bowl

Rinse and chill your favorite in-season fruits in a decorative bowl. Serve with toasted bagels and cream cheese or fresh croissants and softened butter.

Bakin' Bacon

Instead of frying bacon, save the effort and use your oven. About 20 minutes before breakfast is ready, place 6 bacon slices in single layer in baking pan. Heat oven to 325° and cook to desired crispness—about 20-25 minutes. Remove pan with oven mitts, drain bacon on paper towels and serve!

Cinnamon Toast

Heat oven to 250°. Slice 4 pieces of Italian, whole wheat or white bread, and butter on one side. Sprinkle with cinnamon and brown sugar. Place bread slices on baking pan in oven until butter melts. Remove from oven and slice into triangles. Serve immediately.

English Muffins or Toast & Jelly

You've been living on this for years. Toast 'em the way you've always toasted 'em and top with butter and any of your favorite jams and jellies (except KY or naval).

IN CASE OF EMERGENCY

The EATING IN Dinner Dilemma Directory

Jot down these vital numbers now and tack this list to your refrigerator. Or better yet, load the numbers in your speed dialer. You'll be ready to cope, cover up or apologize for just about any cooking disaster you can create.

Domino's: _____

Chinese Takee-Outee: _____

Meals-on-Wheels: _____

Ye Olde Roache Coach: _____

Church of Fried Chicken: _____

Mrs. Paul: _____

Uncle Ben: _____

Dr. Ruth: _____

Salivation Army: _____

Crime Solvers: _____

Ghost Busters: _____

Dial-A-Meal: _____

Dial-A-Prayer: _____

Dial-A-Joke: _____

Victoria's Secret: _____

Insurance Agent: _____

Personal Physician: _____

Legal Aid: _____

Mom: _____

CHAPTER 13

FANCY FOOTWORK

First aid for botched meals and burnt offerings.

Even television personality Chef Tell burns dinner once in a while. But that's little consolation when *your* dinner has melted down—and your date is in the next room eagerly anticipating your gastronomic delight.

There are several sure-fire signals to alert you when your dinner is beyond hope. Learn to identify them:

- Your dog gags from a scrap of the meal you were about to serve your date.
- Your smoke detector blares that your steak is no longer medium-rare (and no longer steak).
- You glance down and see something still stirring in your stir-fry.

Now what do you do?

First, pour her another drink. Then down the rest of the bottle yourself. Now try one of the following solutions:

Grovel and Plead. Beg for help. Maybe she knows how to rescue cremated chicken—or at least salvage the pan.

Bait and Switch. Serve her the appetizer. Then crawl out the bathroom window and dash to the nearest carry-out.

Cover-Up. Scrape off all black-encrusted surfaces. Top with every sauce, dressing or condiment you can find in your refrigerator. Serve with loaves of bread.

Be Honest. Confess your crime and take her out to the best restaurant in town. Attempt to return to your place for dessert.

Be sure to complete the Emergency List on the opposite page so you'll be ready to overcome any cooking disaster at the drop of a pan.

CHAPTER 14

QUICKY CLEAN-UP TIPS

Try these speedy clean-up techniques and you'll be out of the kitchen fast.

U nless you prefer to wash your encrusted dishes with a chisel, the time to clean them is right after dinner.

But at a time like this, who wants to do dishes?

A gracious dinner guest will always offer to help with this unenviable chore. After all, *you* cooked dinner. And you'd really rather be watching WrestleMania.

Now you have a choice. You can accept her generous offer, or continue to impress her with these innovative cleaning techniques that will have both of you relaxing on the couch in no time flat:

- Wrap dishes in tablecloth. Stash under sink.
- Toss pots and pans out window. Unleash dog.
- Put leftovers in manila envelope. Mail to UNICEF.

Here's another suggestion. Rinse your dirty dishes and conceal them under a cover of hot soapy water (or stash them in your dishwasher). Rinse your pots and pans, too. Refrigerate all perishables and left-overs. And unless the odor of fermenting food brings out the beast in her, be sure to twist-tie the Hefty bag.

CHAPTER 15

HOW TO POISON YOUR DATE

Surefire methods to turn your evening—and your stomach— upside-down.

At long last, you and your lovely dinner companion nestle cozily into the couch. Your lips meet. Your bodies intertwine. Your noses quiver, and the sound of loud gastric grumblings fill the air. Suddenly the race to your bathroom is on.

Why did this promising evening end up in the bathroom? Or the emergency room? Because you unwittingly invited an unwanted guest to dinner: Sal Monella. And he's led his raucous band of intestinal terrorists into your meal.

Sal and the gang victimize innocent people who give harmful bacteria free reign on their food. But you can keep Sal and his guerrillas out of your dinner—and your date—simply by being careful. Here's how:

Defrost food in the refrigerator. Frozen food left out on the counter all day is an open invitation to Sal. If you're in a hurry, defrost food by putting it in a waterproof plastic bag in a pot of cold water.

Keep cooked foods away from uncooked foods. Sal salivates when he sees you serving cooked food on the same plate you used to prepare raw food. Always wash plates, knives and preparation surfaces with hot water and soap after each use. Or simply use a different plate.

Refrigerate leftovers at once. Keep Mr. Monella & Co. out of tomorrow's lunch by not letting tonight's dinner sit at room temperature for more than an hour.

Don't use cans that bulge or contain odd-smelling food. It's a sure bet Sal's been camping in there.

Never taste food to see if it's spoiled. That's a job for the neighbor's barking dog. Better yet, when in doubt throw it out.

Always cook pork and chicken thoroughly. You'll kill all the bacteria lurking in there. Undercook it and you'll only get them mad.

Keep your hands clean. Always wash with soap and hot water before and after touching food.

Follow these simple health guidelines and you'll spend your evening embracing your lovely dinner companion—not your porcelain convenience!

Kitchen catastrophes guaranteed to spoil your fun—and your future.

If you can't imagine a kitchen tragedy worse than running out of cold beer, then it's time you doubled your accident insurance. You could easily become a victim of your own carelessness.

Your kitchen is a Pandora's Box of accidents waiting to happen. But with a little foresight, preparation and a smoke detector, you can avoid becoming another emergency room statistic.

For instance, what would you throw on a small grease fire or runaway flambé? Water? Flour? Marshmallows?

None of the above, Scarecrow. If the fire's in a pan, clap on a lid and bring it to the sink, then turn off the appliance. If you have a fire extinguisher, now's the chance you've been waiting for.* Or simply *use handfuls of baking soda*. Never use water or flour.

If the fire is more than you can handle, immediately call the fire department and pull the alarm. Then get your hot buns clothed and out to the street. And bring along the marshmallows.

Other accidents that can happen . . .

Tighten wobbly handles on all pots and pans. Otherwise, your piping hot dinner could end up in someone's lap.

Make sure pan handles are not melting or smelting over lit burners. Keep them turned away from your working and walking areas. And check to see you've turned on the correct burner, or you may be serving fried Teflon for dinner.

Add sufficiently bright lighting over your working area. Be especially careful when you're cutting with sharp knives. Don't lose sight of those sharp knives in soapy dish water either, or you'll be feeling around for missing fingers.

And unless you need to test your smoke detector, always make sure your oven and burners are clean before you use them, and off when you're finished.

*If you need to buy a fire extinguisher, get a Class ABC with at least 2A capacity.

Never cook in the raw.

Always wear an apron.

CHAPTER 16

THE HEIMLICH MANEUVER—

Fist Aid For The Choking Date

This could be your only chance to get your arms around her.

Being alone with a choking person can be a frightening experience. But knowing the proper first aid can save more than just your evening. It can save a life.

And nothing impresses a woman more than saving her life.

Choking occurs most often while eating. And the Heimlich Maneuver is one of the most important advances in emergency care in years. Yet most people don't know how to perform this simple abdominal thrust technique.

People can choke when they are chewing meat poorly, drinking alcohol or talking with their mouths full. So if you gaze lovingly across the table only to see your dinner date inhaling medallions of beef, guzzling your expensive wine and criticizing your cooking, don't hope she chokes. But if she does, you'll now be prepared to deal with this life-threatening emergency.

Universal Choking Signal

How to recognize choking:

- Inability to talk
- Noisy, difficult breathing
- Grasping the throat and pointing at it repeatedly

If she appears to be choking but can breathe and cough forcefully, the coughing is more effective than anything you can do at this time. *Stay calm.* Do not pat her on the back.

Right

Clasp fist in other hand and give 4 sharp, upward thrusts.

Wrong

Try this at the wrong time and you'll get 4 sharp, upward thrusts.

On Your Own

How to react to choking:

Ask her, "Can you speak?" If she cannot speak, or is gasping for breath, or can only cough faintly, administer the Heimlich Maneuver.

How to perform the Heimlich Maneuver:

1. Press the thumb-side of one fist against her abdomen, halfway between her waist and the bottom of her ribs.
2. Grasp your fist with the palm of your other hand and give 4 quick, hard, inward and upward thrusts.

   Adjust the force of your thrusts to the person's size. (If you happen to be involved with a pregnant or obese woman, shift thrusts upward to middle of breastbone.)
3. **Don't give up. Meanwhile, have a neighbor call for medical assistance.**

Continue Heimliching until:

- The object is dislodged and normal breathing resumes, OR
- The person begins to cough forcefully, OR
- The person loses consciousness. This situation requires training in CPR (Cardio-Pulmonary Resuscitation).

If YOU are choking:

- Grasp your throat and point to it (Universal Choking Symbol).
- Pray she knows the Heimlich Maneuver, OR
- Perform the Heimlich Maneuver on yourself. Or lean over the back of a chair, table or counter and push your abdomen down on it.

EATING IN—It's not just a cookbook . . . it's a way of life.

CHAPTER 17

THE FINAL INGREDIENT

Discover the infinite pleasures of EATING IN and experience better dating through cooking.

Every night, while you pace alone in your dreary apartment waiting for the toaster to prepare your Pop Tart dinner, other single men will wine, dine and supine all the attractive women in your town. Not to mention your neighboring cities and bordering states.

Now you can, too—with confidence and ease.

Once you earn your EATING IN Bachelor's Degree, junk food and frozen dinners will become things of your past. And hungry women will become part of your future.

As your cooking improves, word will spread. Your prowess will grow. Your confidence will rise. And before you know it, the right woman will be hungry to eat her way into your heart.

Save enough money EATING IN to take a Club Med vacation!

If you're still not convinced how EATING IN can improve your life, take a closer look at the bottom line. An average dinner date today can easily set you back $40—$60—even $80 and up. Now you can prepare an equivalent meal at home for *less than one-third the cost.*

This means if you opt for the rewards of EATING IN every other week, instead of eating out, you can save as much as $1,000 a year—or more!

Imagine. In just one year you can save enough money EATING IN to buy two VCRs, a wall of CDs or a wide-screen TV—and turn your living room into a total entertainment center. You'll never have to leave home!

Or you can take yourself on an exotic vacation.

Of course, you can still eat out to your heart's content. But now you'll also have the option of EATING IN—and the chance to impress women with your newfound culinary skills.

Think about that the next time your date orders the most expensive entree on the menu. The brainy waitress who memorized your order gets it wrong. The food comes out cold and tasteless. The "background" music drowns out your conversation. She finds the TV over the bar more interesting than you. You can't track down your waiter (or he wants to become your best friend). She bumps into her ex-husband. The couple at the next table keeps mocking your conversation. The waitress interrupts tender, intimate moments to ask if everything's okay. The drinks are watered-down. The table's wobbly. Your seat has bubble gum on it. The arctic blast from the a/c raises more than her dander. The bugs are better fed than you are. You're seated next to Charlie Manson and he's eyeing your woman. Your date never returns from the bathroom. The illegible check seems too expensive. You're short on cash. Your new leather coat disappears from the check room. Your car gets dented in the lot. And then you still have to persuade her to go back to your place.

One thing's for certain. Once you've started EATING IN, you'll never dine so well, pay so little for it, and enjoy so much in return.

So pick a recipe. Pick a date. Pick up the phone. Pick up your groceries. And get cookin'.

Be sure to use the fail-safe checklist at right to avoid needless mistakes and embarrassing moments.

The EATING IN
Last-Minute Checklist

☐ Did you make enough ice?

☐ Is your dinner table set?

☐ Are your "clean" dishes *clean*?

☐ Is the white wine chilling in the refrigerator?

☐ Is the red wine uncorked and breathing?

☐ Are *you* uncorked and breathing?

☐ Is your kitchen counter clear and ready for action?

☐ Are all the ingredients readied for use?

☐ Is this the day she's supposed to come?

☐ Have you thawed your frozen food? And yourself?

☐ Have you taken out the smelly trash?

☐ Are the lights dimmed? Are the candles in place?

☐ Have you lined up your music selections for the evening?

☐ Are there clean towels in the bathroom? Hanging up?

☐ Is there enough toilet paper for her needs (6-roll minimum)?

☐ Is the toilet seat dry? And in the down position?

☐ Is your shower massage set to stun?

☐ Is there soap by the sink? With any recognizable hairs?

☐ Is there a spare contact lens case available?

☐ Is your bed made? Did you use sheets? Are they clean?

☐ Did you hide your loads of dirty laundry? In the car?

☐ Are your girlie magazines stashed away for later?

☐ Are you showered, shaved and dressed?

☐ Is your *Debbie Does Dallas* tape out of the VCR?

☐ Do you have what it takes if she stays till morning?

☐ Does she know you're using this book?

☐ Does her daddy know you're using this book? Is he out of prison?

☐ If this evening works out, do you promise to buy the sequel to this book?

PRIVATE STOCK

Sound advice from the authors' personal collections.

Buy fresh ingredients whenever possible and don't let them sit for more than a day or two. Remember -- today's fresh salad will be floating in its own dressing by week's end.

Always have extra bottles of fine wine on hand. Your guest will be impressed with your collection, especially if you have champagne handy for dessert -- or breakfast.

Try slicing and dicing as much of the ingredients as possible before she arrives, thus giving you more time to spend with her. Otherwise she might be sound asleep when you finally announce dinner.

Warm the fresh bread you serve with dinner and let the butter soften to room temperature. You'll already have a leg up on many restaurants.

Don't overindulge! Heavy, four-course meals will render the two of you bloated, immoble and useless. Lighter meals will keep you frisky.

Class up your evening with a colorful garnish on the dinner plates. Use sprigs of fresh parsley or two green onion stems. Do not use pine cones, hedge clippings or Astroturf.

MUFFY 555-3307

Never use metal utensils on non-stick cookware surfaces unless you prefer to spice up your meal with Teflon topping.

For an evening she'll never forget (or remember), garnish her drink with a long, thin slice of peeled cucumber. We don't know or care why, but cucumber masks the taste of alcohol in a mixed drink, especially gin or rum. Bottoms up!

Disconnect your telephone or turn off the ringer. As much as you'd love to speak with your ex-wife, collection agency or health clinic, let your answering machine take the calls for you.

Pay particular attention to your music and lighting -- you're in your humble abode, not on board the Soooooooooool Train. Turn down the volume, select soothing dinner music and douse the disco lights.

Safe cooking -- like safe sex -- is highly recommended. If nothing else, be sure to wear an apron.

Keep a spare toothbrush sealed in its original factory box. Save the box and reseal for future use.

TERMINOLOGY KEY

Learn to crack the cryptic code of cooking terms without a Captain Cook Decoder Ring.

When it says:	It means:
tsp.	A level teaspoon on your measuring spoon ring (not heaped Nestle's Quik-style).
Tb.	A level tablespoon on your measuring spoon ring (not heaped Scarface-style).
cup	8 fluid ounces in a measuring cup. Does not mean by the mugful or jockful.
garlic clove	One of the individual toes in a garlic bulb.
garlic bulb	The whole clump of cloves. (Do not confuse "bulb" with "clove," or you'll not only repel your date, but fleas, ticks and vampires as well.)
scallion	a.k.a. spring or green onion. Not a short leek or an onion with mold on it.

When it says:	It means:
butter	What Grandma used to churn along with Grandpa. You may substitute equal amounts of margarine for dietary considerations. Measure by using the hash marks on stick and wisely removing paper. Do not substitute love or peanut butter.
vegetable oil	Any of the all-purpose cooking oils you find at the grocery store, including corn, sunflower and salad (but not snake, baby or Ewing).
sauté	To fry quickly in a pan while stirring continuously [saw-tay].
broil	To use the bottom drawer on a gas oven, or the top rack on an electric oven. Put the meat on the broiler *pan* and line the broiler *tray* with aluminum foil for easy clean-up. This method cooks food very quickly at high heat.
bake	To use the large center area of your oven to cook. Hint: empty out dirty dishes and be sure to calibrate to correct temperature with an oven thermometer.

Other cooking terms you'll need to know.

AL DENTE Romantic Italian folk hero who preferred his pasta and women tender but slightly firm to the bite.

BEAT To stir or mix rapidly with even, circular motions using techniques perfected during adolescence.

BOIL To cook liquid rapidly so bubbles will rise and break on the surface. [she was horrified when she saw him sitting in *boiling* bathtub water.]

BROIL To cook by direct heat. [we watched intently as the bikini-clad, oil-slathered sun worshippers *broiled* in the sun.]

CHOP To cut your food into small pieces Chuck Norris style.

COOK 1. (prior to EATING IN) The bachelor science of placing the peanut butter half squarely on the jelly half and tearing into two symmetrical triangles. **2.** (after EATING IN) What you now do in every room of your house.

DASH 1. A very small amount, less than ⅛th teaspoon. **2.** To run to the store for the one ingredient you forgot.

DICE To cut into small cubes to use for cooking or craps.

DISH SOAP A mild cleansing agent perfect for washing your car.

DISH TOWEL [see T-shirt.]

DREDGE To cover food or bodies completely with flour, sugar or water from the Bronx River.

DUST To sprinkle lightly. Customarily delivered by fairies or angels.

FREEZER A dinner date that needs defrosting.

GARBAGE PALE The color she'll turn upon smelling that heap of trash in the kitchen.

GRATE To rub solid food against a metal surface that has sharp-edged holes, reducing food and fingers to thin shreds.

KITCHEN 1. (prior to EATING IN) A built-in depository for empty beer bottles, pizza boxes and yellow waxy build-up. **2.** (after EATING IN) A room that rivals your bedroom for fun.

KITCHEN FLOOR A colorful and often odoriferous canvas of food substances created over the years by numerous tenants and pets.

KITCHEN SINK The beginning of the food chain. The end of your appetite.

PATÉ The only place you'll see this quiche-y term in this book.

PEANUT BUTTER 'n' JELLY The bachelor meal most likely to be eaten when the toaster oven is broken. [see *toaster oven*]

PINCH The amount you can safely squeeze between your thumb and forefinger.

PREHEAT 1. To heat oven or griddle to desired temperature for cooking. **2.** To ply dinner date with drinks upon arrival.

SCORE To slash the side of meat to prevent curling. [she told him if he wanted to *score*, he could do it on the tennis court.]

SILVERWARE DRAWER A storage space where your chances of finding a matching set of utensils are slimmer than winning the lottery.

SPICE RACK A stand designed to conveniently display a typical bachelor's spice collection: salt, pepper and carry-out packets of soy sauce.

Cooking Terms. . .continued

SPONGE A dry, brittle object that when dampened, releases toxic odors perfect for ridding a house of roaches, mice and guests.

T-SHIRT [See dish towel.]

TOAST Bread that's not completely burnt.

TOASTER OVEN The only working kitchen appliance in a typical bachelor's apartment.

TUPPERWARE A final resting place for formerly edible foods.

UNDER THE SINK The place where things end up when the trash and sink are full.

WHISK To whip. [she *whisked* him into submission.]

PERFECT MEASUREMENTS

Use this handy conversion table to solve all your cooking, science, math and philosophical needs.

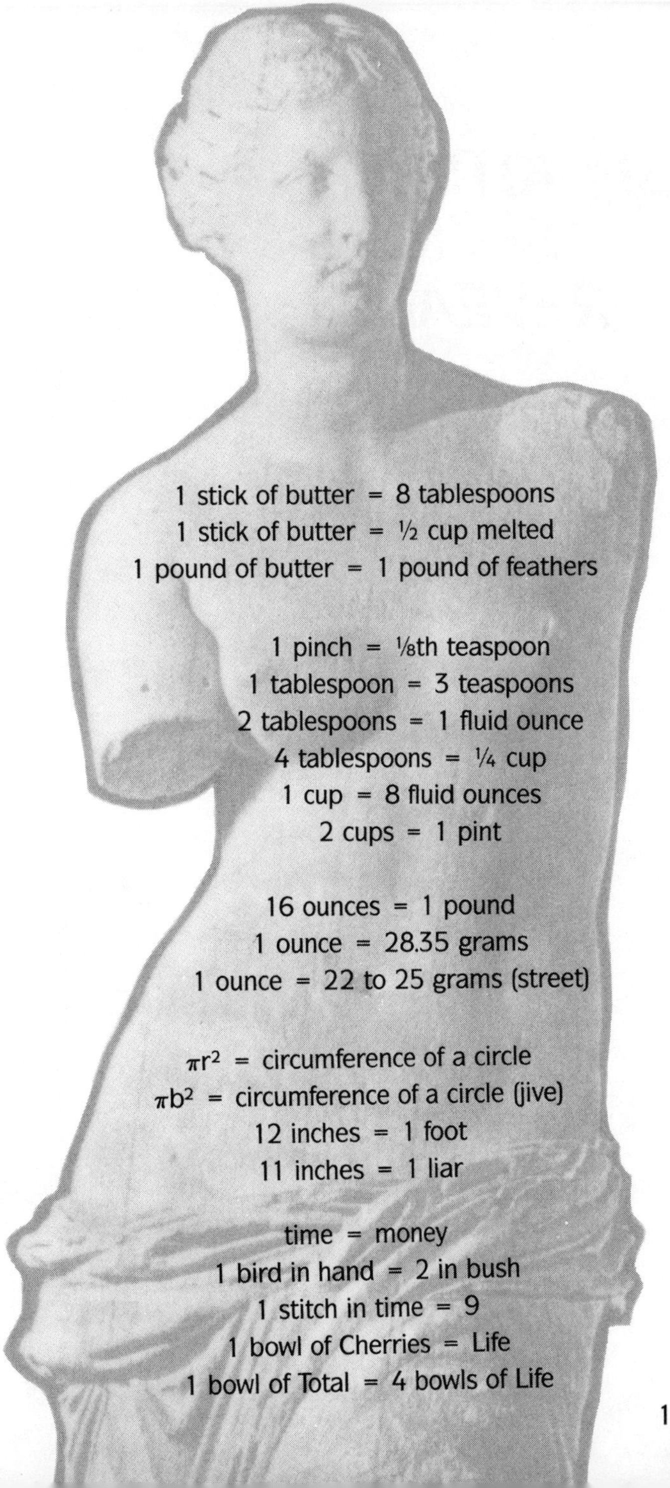

1 stick of butter = 8 tablespoons
1 stick of butter = ½ cup melted
1 pound of butter = 1 pound of feathers

1 pinch = ⅛th teaspoon
1 tablespoon = 3 teaspoons
2 tablespoons = 1 fluid ounce
4 tablespoons = ¼ cup
1 cup = 8 fluid ounces
2 cups = 1 pint

16 ounces = 1 pound
1 ounce = 28.35 grams
1 ounce = 22 to 25 grams (street)

πr^2 = circumference of a circle
πb^2 = circumference of a circle (jive)
12 inches = 1 foot
11 inches = 1 liar

time = money
1 bird in hand = 2 in bush
1 stitch in time = 9
1 bowl of Cherries = Life
1 bowl of Total = 4 bowls of Life

The authors would like to thank their math and science teachers, who over the years imparted much of the otherwise useless information shown here.

SIX KITCHEN SECRETS REVEALED

These handy illustrated techniques will help you look as good as you cook.

Mincing Garlic

Make sure you know the difference between a bulb and a clove.

Lightly crush clove under the broad side of a knife. Remove all papery gift wrapping from around clove until you reach the smooth, shiny flesh.

Mince clove (chop finely) or crush in garlic press—or save yourself all the hassle and buy one of those tiny jars of pre-crushed garlic.

Skinning Scallions

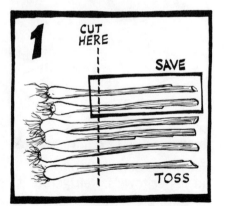

Trim green leafy tops off scallions 2 inches from bulb. (Save two tops for an impressive dinner plate garnish.)

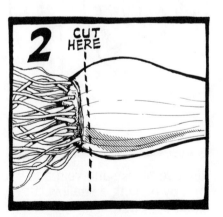

Amputate the roots.

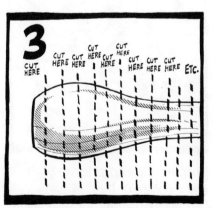

Peel off outer layer of onion and slice remaining bulb into disks. Both you and the scallions are ready to cook.

Preparing Mushrooms

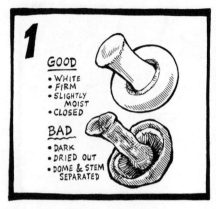

Buy only fresh mushrooms.

Use a dampened paper towel or cloth to wipe dirt and grit off mushrooms.

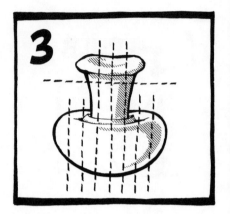

Trim off bottom of stem. Then if recipe requires, cut lengthwise along dotted lines about ⅛-inch thick.

Undressing Shrimp

Prepare shrimp prior to your guest's arrival by first ruthlessly ripping off their little legs, outer shells and tails (and heads if they got 'em).

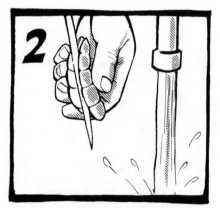

Remove black sand vein and guts by making a shallow cut along the entire length of the shrimp's back with a paring knife. Rinse it all out under cold water.

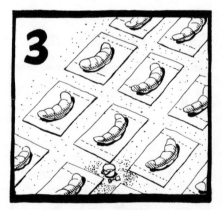

Set undressed shrimp to dry on paper towels. Refrigerate if preparing shrimp ahead of time. Then wash hands with water and lemon juice lest your date wonder what you've been up to.

Steaming Vegetables

Open steamer and place in medium or large saucepan. Add water till level is just *below* bottom of steamer. Bring water to boil.

Place rinsed and cut-up vegetables on steamer, cover pan and cook until tender. Don't overcook!

Unless your smoke detector needs testing, don't allow water to boil dry.

Cracking Eggs

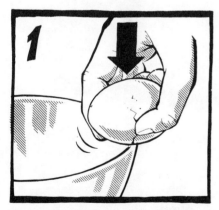

Strike middle of egg sharply on the edge of a pan or bowl. Hold onto both halves of shell, and let contents slip out into bowl.

Or, hold egg in palm of hand and crack it lightly with the back end of a knife.

After some practice, you'll be able to crack and separate the shells with one hand.

You've Graduated...

THE FRY-BY-NIGHT COOKING SCHOOL AND DIPLOMA MILL

Confers on:

_____

The Degree Of

BACHELOR OF EATING IN

For having successfully classed up his kitchen and his act
by mastering the recipes and precepts necessary for
Extraordinary Dining and Entertaining at home.

Awarded: The _____ Day of _____, 19 _____

Presented by:
The Founders of Fry-By-Night Cooking School

_____
Okra Winfrey
Doctor of Eating In

Vinnie Garrette
Doctor of Eating In

© 1988 Corkscrew Press

**Your diploma comes direct from the Fry-By-Night
Cooking School & Diploma Mill.™**

. . . *Now You Can Prove It.*

Send for your Official EATING IN Bachelor's Degree—
Guaranteed to class up your kitchen and your act.

Show her you're an accomplished EATING IN chef before she gets her first taste. Proudly display your official-looking Bachelor's Degree— suitable for framing or hanging on your refrigerator. It's the certificate that says, "You won't be cooking fish sticks *à la mode* tonight."

YES! Send me an Official-Looking EATING IN Bachelor's Degree. I've enclosed $2 plus $1 postage and handling.

Name _____

Address _____

City _____ State _____ Zip _____

Send check or money order only! Do not send cash! Make your check payable to: CorkScrew Press. Please allow 4–6 weeks for delivery.

Maryland residents: You must add 5% sales tax or else.

Mail your order to:

    EATING IN BACHELOR'S DEGREE
    CorkScrew Press
    P.O. Box 2691
    Silver Spring, MD 20902-0115

How Was It For You?

Send us your funniest, craziest, sexiest, most outrageous or tasteless EATING IN escapade.

Here's your chance to prove that truth can be stranger than fiction: tell us what happened on your EATING IN date. Did it sizzle—or fizzle? Did you bake—or shake? Did your dinner broil—or just spoil?

Write down your personal EATING IN experience and mail it to us today. Be sure to include your name, address and phone number if you dare. And ask your dinner companion to tell us how it was for her (include her phone number, too.)

The most outrageous story each month will win a free EATING IN diploma (*summa cum laude* edition) and an autographed copy of EATING IN!

Send your real-life story to:

ADVENTURES IN EATING IN
CorkScrew Press
P.O. Box 2691
Silver Spring, MD 20902

Earn Big Bucks EATING IN!

Send us your best recipe.
If we publish it, we'll pay you $25.

Carry on the quest to save mankind from terminal junk food diets. Send us your favorite, easy-to-prepare recipes—the ones with that take little effort and deliver big taste.

If your recipe is selected for publication you'll get $25, full credit (to impress your friends), and a free copy of EATING IN signed by the authors.

Your recipe must meet these requirements:

- easy-to-find ingredients
- easy-to-follow instructions
- no fancy equipment
- minimum effort/maximum taste
- yields two servings

Here's what we're looking for: main and side dishes, appetizers, desserts, ethnic favorites, momma's secrets, local delicacies, brunches, microwave meals and barbecued beauties.

Here are the rules:

1. *Send only original material please.* No copyrighted recipes copied right outta someone else's cookbook.

2. List all the ingredients, and write down the recipe steps as clearly as possible.

3. Be sure to include your name, address and phone number (single women must enclose recent photo).

Send your recipes to:

HOT RECIPES ENCLOSED!
CorkScrew Press
P.O. Box 2691
Silver Spring, MD 20902

Do You Have Friends*
Who Need EATING IN?

*(or sons, neighbors, brothers, co-workers, inmates...?)

Let Your Friends Try EATING IN Themselves.

Rescue your bachelor friends from endless frozen pizza dinners and expensive, lackluster dates with the gift of EATING IN—*The Official Single Man's Cookbook.*

For just under ten bucks, you'll be credited with giving them a new outlook on life. A healthier diet. And the key to better dating through cooking.

Don't wait another minute to give your friends the cooking skills they need. They're probably snarfing down a rancid can of tunafish right now.